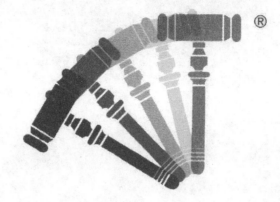

Casenote™ Legal Briefs

CONFLICTS

Keyed to
Brilmayer and Goldsmith's
Conflict of Laws: Cases and Materials

Aspen Publishers, Inc.
New York, Gaithersburg

Copyright © 2002 by Aspen Law & Business
A Division of Aspen Publishers, Inc.
A Wolters Kluwer Company
www.aspenpublishers.com

Permissions
Aspen Law & Business
1185 Avenue of the Americas
New York, NY 10036

Printed in the United States of America.

ISBN 0-7355-3552-3

1 2 3 4 5 6 7 8 9 0

FORMAT FOR THE CASENOTE LEGAL BRIEF

PARTY ID: Quick identification of the relationship between the parties.

NATURE OF CASE: This section identifies the form of action (e.g., breach of contract, negligence, battery), the type of proceeding (e.g., demurrer, appeal from trial court's jury instructions) or the relief sought (e.g., damages, injunction, criminal sanctions).

FACT SUMMARY: This is included to refresh the student's memory and can be used as a quick reminder of the facts.

CONCISE RULE OF LAW: Summarizes the general principle of law that the case illustrates. It may be used for instant recall of the court's holding and for classroom discussion or home review.

FACTS: This section contains all relevant facts of the case, including the contentions of the parties and the lower court holdings. It is written in a logical order to give the student a clear understanding of the case. The plaintiff and defendant are identified by their proper names throughout and are always labeled with a (P) or (D).

ISSUE: The issue is a concise question that brings out the essence of the opinion as it relates to the section of the casebook in which the case appears. Both substantive and procedural issues are included if relevant to the decision.

HOLDING AND DECISION: This section offers a clear and in-depth discussion of the rule of the case and the court's rationale. It is written in easy-to-understand language and answers the issue(s) presented by applying the law to the facts of the case. When relevant, it includes a thorough discussion of the exceptions to the case as listed by the court, any major cites to other cases on point, and the names of the judges who wrote the decisions.

CONCURRENCE / DISSENT: All concurrences and dissents are briefed whenever they are included by the casebook editor.

EDITOR'S ANALYSIS: This last paragraph gives the student a broad understanding of where the case "fits in" with other cases in the section of the book and with the entire course. It is a hornbook-style discussion indicating whether the case is a majority or minority opinion and comparing the principal case with other cases in the casebook. It may also provide analysis from restatements, uniform codes, and law review articles. The editor's analysis will prove to be invaluable to classroom discussion.

QUICKNOTES: Conveniently defines legal terms found in the case and summarizes the nature of any statutes, codes, or rules referred to in the text.

PALSGRAF v. LONG ISLAND R.R. CO.
Injured bystander (P) v. Railroad company (D)
N.Y. Ct. App., 248 N.Y. 339, 162 N.E. 99 (1928).

NATURE OF CASE: Appeal from judgment affirming verdict for plaintiff seeking damages for personal injury.

FACT SUMMARY: Helen Palsgraf (P) was injured on R.R.'s (D) train platform when R.R.'s (D) guard helped a passenger aboard a moving train, causing his package to fall on the tracks. The package contained fireworks which exploded, creating a shock that tipped a scale onto Palsgraf (P).

CONCISE RULE OF LAW: The risk reasonably to be perceived defines the duty to be obeyed.

FACTS: Helen Palsgraf (P) purchased a ticket to Rockaway Beach from R.R. (D) and was waiting on the train platform. As she waited, two men ran to catch a train that was pulling out from the platform. The first man jumped aboard, but the second man, who appeared as if he might fall, was helped aboard by the guard on the train who had kept the door open so they could jump aboard. A guard on the platform also helped by pushing him onto the train. The man was carrying a package wrapped in newspaper. In the process, the man dropped his package, which fell on the tracks. The package contained fireworks and exploded. The shock of the explosion was apparently of great enough strength to tip over some scales at the other end of the platform, which fell on Palsgraf (P) and injured her. A jury awarded her damages, and R.R. (D) appealed.

ISSUE: Does the risk reasonably to be perceived define the duty to be obeyed?

HOLDING AND DECISION: (Cardozo, C.J.) Yes. The risk reasonably to be perceived defines the duty to be obeyed. If there is no foreseeable hazard to the injured party as the result of a seemingly innocent act, the act does not become a tort because it happened to be a wrong as to another. If the wrong was not willful, the plaintiff must show that the act as to her had such great and apparent possibilities of danger as to entitle her to protection. Negligence in the abstract is not enough upon which to base liability. Negligence is a relative concept, evolving out of the common law doctrine of trespass on the case. To establish liability, the defendant must owe a legal duty of reasonable care to the injured party. A cause of action in tort will lie where harm, though unintended, could have been averted or avoided by observance of such a duty. The scope of the duty is limited by the range of danger that a reasonable person could foresee. In this case, there was nothing to suggest from the appearance of the parcel or otherwise that the parcel contained fireworks. The guard could not reasonably have had any warning of a threat to Palsgraf (P), and R.R. (D) therefore cannot be held liable. Judgment is reversed in favor of R.R. (D).

DISSENT: (Andrews, J.) The concept that there is no negligence unless R.R. (D) owes a legal duty to take care as to Palsgraf (P) herself is too narrow. Everyone owes to the world at large the duty of refraining from those acts that may unreasonably threaten the safety of others. If the guard's action was negligent as to those nearby, it was also negligent as to those outside what might be termed the "danger zone." For Palsgraf (P) to recover, R.R.'s (D) negligence must have been the proximate cause of her injury, a question of fact for the jury.

EDITOR'S ANALYSIS: The majority defined the limit of the defendant's liability in terms of the danger that a reasonable person in defendant's situation would have perceived. The dissent argued that the limitation should not be placed on liability, but rather on damages. Judge Andrews suggested that only injuries that would not have happened but for R.R.'s (D) negligence should be compensable. Both the majority and dissent recognized the policy-driven need to limit liability for negligent acts, seeking, in the words of Judge Andrews, to define a framework "that will be practical and in keeping with the general understanding of mankind." The Restatement (Second) of Torts has accepted Judge Cardozo's view.

QUICKNOTES
FORESEEABILITY – The reasonable anticipation that damage is a likely result from certain acts or omissions.
NEGLIGENCE - Failure to exercise that degree of care which a person of ordinary prudence would exercise under similar circumstances.
PROXIMATE CAUSE – Something which in natural and continuous sequence, unbroken by any new intervening cause, produces an event, and without which the injury would not have occurred.

Note to Students

Aspen Publishers is proud to offer *Casenote Legal Briefs*–continuing thirty years of publishing America's best-selling legal briefs.

Casenote Legal Briefs are designed to help you save time when briefing assigned cases. Organized under convenient headings, they show you how to abstract the basic facts and holdings from the text of the actual opinions handed down by the courts. Used as part of a rigorous study regime, they can help you spend more time analyzing and critiquing points of law than on copying out bits and pieces of judicial opinions into your notebook or outline.

Casenote Legal Briefs should never be used as a substitute for assigned casebook readings. They work best when read as a follow-up to reviewing the underlying opinions themselves. Students who try to avoid reading and digesting the judicial opinions in their casebooks or on-line sources will end up shortchanging themselves in the long run. The ability to absorb, critique, and restate the dynamic and complex elements of case law decisions is crucial to your success in law school and beyond. It cannot be developed vicariously.

Casenote Legal Briefs represent but one of the many offerings in Aspen's Study Aid Timeline, which includes:

- Casenotes *Legal Briefs*
- Emanuel *Outlines*
- *Examples & Explanations* Series
- *Introduction to Law* Series
- Emanuel *Law in A Flash* Flashcards
- Emanuel *CrunchTime* Series

Each of these series is designed to provide you with easy-to-understand explanations of complex points of law. Each volume offers guidance on the principles of legal analysis and, consulted regularly, will hone your ability to spot relevant issues. We have titles that will help you prepare for class, prepare for your exams, and enhance your general comprehension of the law along the way.

To find out more about Aspen Study Aid publications, visit us on-line at www.aspenpublishers.com or e-mail us at legaledu@aspenpubl.com. We'll be happy to assist you.

Free access to Briefs and Updates on-line!

Download the cases you want in your notes or outlines using the full cut-and-paste feature accompanying our on-line briefs. On-line briefs will also contain the latest updates. Please fill out this form for full access to these useful features. No photocopies of this form will be accepted.

① Name: _____ Phone: (___) _____

Address: _____ Apt.: _____

City: _____ State: _____ ZIP Code: _____

Law School: _____ Year (circle one): 1st 2nd 3rd

② Cut out the UPC found on the lower left-hand corner of the back cover of this book. Staple the UPC inside this box. Only the original UPC from the book cover will be accepted. (No photocopies or store stickers are allowed.)

Attach UPC inside this box.

③ E-mail:_____ (Print LEGIBLY or you may not get access!

④ Title (course subject) of this book _____

⑤ Used with which casebook (provide author's name): _____

⑥ Mail the completed form to: Aspen Publishers, Inc.
                                    Legal Education Division
                                    Casenote On-line Access
                                    1185 Avenue of the Americas
                                    New York, NY 10036

I understand that on-line access is granted solely to the purchaser of this book for the academic year in which it was purchased. Any other usage is not authorized and will result in immediate termination of access. Sharing of codes is strictly prohibited.

_____
Signature

Upon receipt of this completed form, you will be e-mailed codes so that you may access the Briefs and Updates for this Casenote Legal Brief. On-line Briefs and Updates may not be available for all titles. For a full list of available titles please check www.aspenpublishers.com/casenotes.

HOW TO BRIEF A CASE

A. DECIDE ON A FORMAT AND STICK TO IT

Structure is essential to a good brief. It enables you to arrange systematically the related parts that are scattered throughout most cases, thus making manageable and understandable what might otherwise seem to be an endless and unfathomable sea of information. There are, of course, an unlimited number of formats that can be utilized. However, it is best to find one that suits your needs and stick to it. Consistency breeds both efficiency and the security that when called upon you will know where to look in your brief for the information you are asked to give.

Any format, as long as it presents the essential elements of a case in an organized fashion, can be used. Experience, however, has led *Casenotes* to develop and utilize the following format because of its logical flow and universal applicability.

NATURE OF CASE: This is a brief statement of the legal character and procedural status of the case (e.g., "Appeal of a burglary conviction").

There are many different alternatives open to a litigant dissatisfied with a court ruling. The key to determining which one has been used is to discover *who is asking this court for what.*

This first entry in the brief should be kept as *short as possible.* The student should use the court's terminology if the student understands it. But since jurisdictions vary as to the titles of pleadings, the best entry is the one that apprises the student of who wants what in this proceeding, not the one that sounds most like the court's language.

CONCISE RULE OF LAW: A statement of the general principle of law that the case illustrates (e.g., "An acceptance that varies any term of the offer is considered a rejection and counteroffer").

Determining the rule of law of a case is a procedure similar to determining the issue of the case. Avoid being fooled by red herrings; there may be a few rules of law mentioned in the case excerpt, but usually only one is *the* rule with which the casebook editor is concerned. The techniques used to locate the issue, described below, may also be utilized to find the rule of law. Generally, your best guide is simply the chapter heading. It is a clue to the point the casebook editor seeks to make and should be kept in mind when reading every case in the respective section.

FACTS: A synopsis of only the essential facts of the case, i.e., those bearing upon or leading up to the issue.

The facts entry should be a short statement of the events and transactions that led one party to initiate legal proceedings against another in the first place. While some cases conveniently state the salient facts at the beginning of the decision, in other instances they will have to be culled from hiding places throughout the text, even from concurring and dissenting opinions. Some of the "facts" will often be in dispute and should be so noted. Conflicting evidence may be briefly pointed up. "Hard" facts must be included. Both must be *relevant* in order to be listed in the facts entry. It is impossible to tell what is relevant until the entire case is read, as the ultimate determination of the rights and liabilities of the parties may turn on something buried deep in the opinion.

The facts entry should never be longer than one to three *short* sentences.

It is often helpful to identify the role played by a party in a given context. For example, in a construction contract case the identification of a party as the "contractor" or "builder" alleviates the need to tell that that party was the one who was supposed to have built the house.

It is always helpful, and a good general practice, to identify the "plaintiff" and the "defendant." This may seem elementary and uncomplicated, but, especially in view of the creative editing practiced by some casebook editors, it is sometimes a difficult or even impossible task. Bear in mind that the *party presently* seeking something from this court may not be the plaintiff, and that sometimes only the cross-claim of a defendant is treated in the excerpt. Confusing or misaligning the parties can ruin your analysis and understanding of the case.

ISSUE: A statement of the general legal question answered by or illustrated in the case. For clarity, the issue is best put in the form of a question capable of a "yes" or "no" answer. In reality, the issue is simply the Concise Rule of Law put in the form of a question (e.g., "May an offer be accepted by performance?").

The major problem presented in discerning what is *the* issue in the case is that an opinion usually purports to raise and answer several questions. However, except for rare cases, only one such question is really the issue in the case. Collateral issues not necessary to the resolution of the matter in controversy are handled by the court by language known as *"obiter dictum"* or merely *"dictum."* While dicta may be included later in the brief, it has no place under the issue heading.

To find the issue, the student again asks *who wants what* and then goes on to ask *why did that party succeed or fail in getting it.* Once this is determined, the "why" should be turned into a question.

The complexity of the issues in the cases will vary, but in all cases a single-sentence question should sum up the issue. *In a few cases,* there will be two, or even more rarely, three issues of equal importance to the resolution of the case. Each should be expressed in a single-sentence question.

Since many issues are resolved by a court in coming to a final disposition of a case, the casebook editor will reproduce the portion of the opinion containing the issue or issues most relevant to the area of law under scrutiny. A noted law professor gave this advice: "Close the book; look at the title on the cover." Chances are, if it is Property, the student need not concern himself with whether, for example, the federal government's treatment of the plaintiff's land really raises a federal question sufficient to support jurisdiction on this ground in federal court.

The same rule applies to chapter headings designating sub-areas within the subjects. They tip the student off as to what the text is designed to teach. The cases are arranged in a casebook to show a progression or development of the law, so that the preceding cases may also help.

It is also most important to remember to *read the notes and questions* at the end of a case to determine what the editors wanted the student to have gleaned from it.

HOLDING AND DECISION: This section should succinctly explain the rationale of the court in arriving at its decision. In capsulizing the "reasoning" of the court, it should always include an application of the general rule or rules of law to the specific facts of the case. Hidden justifications come to light in this entry; the reasons for the state of the law, the public policies, the biases and prejudices, those considerations that influence the justices' thinking and, ultimately, the outcome of the case. At the end, there should be a short indication of the disposition or procedural resolution of the case (e.g., "Decision of the trial court for Mr. Smith (P) reversed").

The foregoing format is designed to help you "digest" the reams of case material with which you will be faced in your law school career. Once mastered by practice, it will place at your fingertips the information the authors of your casebooks have sought to impart to you in case-by-case illustration and analysis.

B. BE AS ECONOMICAL AS POSSIBLE IN BRIEFING CASES

Once armed with a format that encourages succinctness, it is as important to be economical with regard to the time spent on the actual reading of the case as it is to be economical in the writing of the brief itself. This does not mean "skimming" a case. Rather, it means reading the case with an "eye" trained to recognize into which "section" of your brief a particular passage or line fits and having a system for quickly and precisely marking the case so that the passages fitting any one particular part of the brief can be easily identified and brought together in a concise and accurate manner when the brief is actually written.

It is of no use to simply repeat everything in the opinion of the court; the student should only record enough information to trigger his or her recollection of what the court said. Nevertheless, an accurate statement of the "law of the case," i.e., the legal principle applied to the facts, is absolutely essential to class preparation and to learning the law under the case method.

To that end, it is important to develop a "shorthand" that you can use to make margin notations. These notations will tell you at a glance in which section of the brief you will be placing that particular passage or portion of the opinion.

Some students prefer to underline all the salient portions of the opinion (with a pencil or colored underliner marker), making marginal notations as they go along. Others prefer the color-coded method of under-lining, utilizing different colors of markers to underline the salient portions of the case, each separate color being used to represent a different section of the brief. For example, blue underlining could be used for passages relating to the concise rule of law, yellow for those relating to the issue, and green for those relating to the holding and decision, etc. While it has its advocates, the color-coded method can be confusing and time-consuming (all that time spent on changing colored markers). Furthermore, it can interfere with the continuity and concentration many students deem essential to the reading of a case for maximum comprehension. In the end, however, it is a matter of personal preference and style. Just remember, whatever method you use, underlining must be used sparingly or its value is lost.

For those who take the marginal notation route, an efficient and easy method is to go along underlining the key portions of the case and placing in the margin alongside them the following "markers" to indicate where a particular passage or line "belongs" in the brief you will write:

N   (NATURE OF CASE)
CR   (CONCISE RULE OF LAW)
I   (ISSUE)
HC   (HOLDING AND DECISION, relates to the CONCISE RULE OF LAW behind the decision)
HR   (HOLDING AND DECISION, gives the RATIONALE or reasoning behind the decision)
HA   (HOLDING AND DECISION, APPLIES the general principle(s) of law to the facts of the case to arrive at the decision)

Remember that a particular passage may well contain information necessary to more than one part of your brief, in which case you simply note that in the margin. If you are using the color-coded underlining method instead of margin notation, simply make asterisks or checks in the margin next to the passage in question in the colors that indicate the additional sections of the brief where it might be utilized.

The economy of utilizing "shorthand" in marking cases for briefing can be maintained in the actual brief writing process itself by utilizing "law student shorthand" within the brief. There are many commonly used words and phrases for which abbreviations can be substituted in your briefs (and in your class notes also). You can develop abbreviations that are personal to you and which will save you a lot of time. A reference list of briefing abbreviations will be found elsewhere in this book.

C. USE BOTH THE BRIEFING PROCESS AND THE BRIEF AS A LEARNING TOOL

Now that you have a format and the tools for briefing cases efficiently, the most important thing is to make the time spent in briefing profitable to you and to make the most advantageous use of the briefs you create. Of course, the briefs are invaluable for classroom reference when you are called upon to explain or analyze a particular case. However, they are also useful in reviewing for exams. A quick glance at the fact summary should bring the case to mind, and a rereading of the concise rule of law should enable you to go over the underlying legal concept in your mind, how it was applied in that particular case, and how it might apply in other factual settings.

As to the value to be derived from engaging in the briefing process itself, there is an immediate benefit that arises from being forced to sift through the essential facts and reasoning from the court's opinion and to succinctly express them in your own words in your brief. The process ensures that you understand the case and the point that it illustrates, and that means you will be ready to absorb further analysis and information brought forth in class. It also ensures you will have something to say when called upon in class. The briefing process helps develop a mental agility for getting to the *gist* of a case and for identifying, expounding on, and applying the legal concepts and issues found there. Of most immediate concern, that is the mental process on which you must rely in taking law school examinations. Of more lasting concern, it is also the mental process upon which a lawyer relies in serving his clients and in making his living.

ABBREVIATIONS FOR BRIEFING

acceptance	acp	offer	O
affirmed	aff	offeree	OE
answer	ans	offeror	OR
assumption of risk	a/r	ordinance	ord
attorney	atty	pain and suffering	p/s
beyond a reasonable doubt	b/r/d	parol evidence	p/e
bona fide purchaser	BFP	plaintiff	P
breach of contract	br/k	prima facie	p/f
cause of action	c/a	probably cause	p/c
common law	c/l	proximate cause	px/c
Constitution	Con	real property	r/p
constitutional	con	reasonable doubt	r/d
contract	K	reasonable man	r/m
contributory negligence	c/n	rebuttable presumption	rb/p
cross	x	remanded	rem
cross-complaint	x/c	res ipsa loquitur	RIL
cross-examination	x/ex	respondeat superior	r/s
cruel and unusual punishment	c/u/p	Restatement	RS
defendant	D	reversed	rev
dismissed	dis	Rule Against Perpetuities	RAP
double jeopardy	d/j	search and seizure	s/s
due process	d/p	search warrant	s/w
equal protection	e/p	self-defense	s/d
equity	eq	specific performance	s/p
evidence	ev	statute of limitations	S/L
exclude	exc	statute of frauds	S/F
exclusionary rule	exc/r	statute	S
felony	f/n	summary judgment	s/j
freedom of speech	f/s	tenancy in common	t/c
good faith	g/f	tenancy at will	t/w
habeas corpus	h/c	tenant	t
hearsay	hr	third party	TP
husband	H	third party beneficiary	TPB
in loco parentis	ILP	transferred intent	TI
injunction	inj	unconscionable	uncon
inter vivos	I/v	unconstitutional	unconst
joint tenancy	j/t	undue influence	u/e
judgment	judgt	Uniform Commercial Code	UCC
jurisdiction	jur	unilateral	uni
last clear chance	LCC	vendee	VE
long-arm statute	LAS	vendor	VR
majority view	maj	versus	v
meeting of minds	MOM	void for vagueness	VFV
minority view	min	weight of the evidence	w/e
Miranda warnings	Mir/w	weight of authority	w/a
Miranda rule	Mir/r	wife	W
negligence	neg	with	w/
notice	ntc	within	w/i
nuisance	nus	without prejudice	w/o/p
obligation	ob	without	w/o
obscene	obs	wrongful death	wr/d

TABLE OF CASES

A

Air Crash Disaster Near New Orleans, In re 96
Alabama Great Southern Railroad v. Carroll 5
Allstate Ins. Co. v. Hague 65
America Online, Inc. v. National Health Care
    Discount, Inc. 132
America Online, Inc. v. Superior Court of Alameda
County 131
America Library Association v. Pataki 136
Asahi Metal Industry Co., Ltd. v. Superior Court
    of California, Solano County 86
Austin v. New Hampshire 71

B

Babcock v. Jackson 37
Baker v. General Motors Corp. 108
Banco Nacional de Cuba v. Sabbatino 118
Banek, Inc. v. Yogurt Ventures U.S.A., Inc. 49
Bernhard v. Harrah's Club 45
Bernkrant v. Fowler 43
Bremen, The v. Zapata Off-Shore Co. 77
Brown-Forman Distillers Corp. v. New York State
    Liquor Authority 73
Burnham v. Superior Court of California 83
Burr v. Beckler 13

C

CTS Corp. v. Dynamics Corporation of America 74
Caesars World Inc. v. Caesars-Palace.com 130
Carnival Cruise Lines, Inc. v. Shute 78
Caspi v. The Microsoft Network, LLC 130
Clay v. Sun Insurance Office, Ltd. 64
Clearfield Trust Co. v. United States 98
Cybersell, Inc. v. Cybersell, Inc. 128

D

Damato, In re Estate of 22
Davis, United States v. 125
Duke v. Housen 27
Durfee v. Duke 103

E

EEOC v. Arabian American Oil Co. 119
Erie Railroad Co. v. Tompkins 91
Estin v. Estin 112

F

Fall v. Eastin 104
Fauntleroy v. Lum 106
Ferens v. John Deere Co. 94
Filartiga v. Pena-Irala 122

G

G.D. Searle & Co. v. Cohn 72
Global Financial Corp. v. Triare Corp. 55
Grant v. McAuliffe 26

H

Haag v. Barnes 36
Hartford Fire Insurance Co. v. California 121
Haumschild v. Continental Casualty Co. 21
Helicopteros Nacionales de Columbia, S.A.
    v. Hall 82
Holzer v. Deutsche Reichsbahn-Gesellschaft 29
Home Insurance Co. v. Dick 61
Hughes v. Fetter 68
Hurtado v. Superior Court 44
Hutchinson v. Ross 18

I

Illinois v. City of Milwaukee 99
Insurance Corporation of Ireland v. Compagnie
    des Bauxites de Guinee 81
Irving Trust Co. v. Maryland Casualty Co. 16

J

Jeri-Jo Knitwear, Inc. v. Club Italia, Inc. 134
Johnson v. Muelberger 114

K

Kalb v. Feuerstein 105
Kipin Industries, Inc. v. Van Deilen
    International, Inc. 50
Klaxon v. Stentor Electric Mfg. Co. 92
Kulko v. Superior Court 85

L

Lanham v. Lanham 10
Lauritzen v. Larsen 120
Ledesma v. Jack Stewart Produce, Inc. 54
Licra and UEJF v. Yahoo! Inc. 135
Lilienthal v. Kaufman 42
Linn v. Employers Reinsurance Corp. 8

M

Marchlik v. Coronet Insurance Co. 28
Marra v. Bushee 6
Matusevitch v. Ivanovich 126
May v. Anderson 113
May's Estate, In re, ... 11
McDermott Inc. v. Lewis 17
Milkovich v. Saari 46
Morson v. Second National Bank of Boston 20

N

Nedlloyd Lines B.V. v. Superior Court of
  San Mateo County Seawinds Ltd. 48
Neumeier v. Kuehner 39
Nevada v. Hall 70
New York, People of the State of v. World Interactive
  Gaming Corp. 133

O

O'Leary v. Illinois Terminal Railroad 25

P

Pacific Employers Insurance Co. v. Industrial
  Accident Commission 62
Padula v. Lilarn Properties Corporation 41
Paper Products Co. v. Doggrell 30
Paul v. National Life 56
Pfau v. Trent Aluminum Co. 52
Phillips Petroleum Co. v. Shutts 66, 80
Phillips v. General Motors Corp. 47
Poole v. Perkins 7

R

Reich v. Purcell 51
Richards v. United States 53
Rodriguez Diaz v. Sierra Martinez 10

S

Salavarria v. National Car Rental System, Inc. 57
Sampson v. Channell 24
Schultz v. Boy Scouts of America, Inc. 40
Semtek Int'l Inc. v. Lockheed Martin Corp. 97
Shaffer v. Heitner 87

Starmedia Network, Inc. v. Star Media, Inc. 129
Sternberg v. O'Neil 79, 88
Stewart Organization, Inc. v. Ricoh Corp 95
Sun Oil Co. v. Wortman 67

T

Thomas v. Washington Gas Light Co. 107
Thompson v. Kyle 14
Tidewater Oil Co. v. Waller 31
Tooker v. Lopez 38
Treinies v. Sunshine Mining Co. 111

U

Union National Bank v. Lamb 109
University of Chicago v. Dater 23

V

Van Dusen v. Barrack 93
Vanderpoel v. Gorman 15
Verdugo-Urquidez, United States v., ... 135

W

Washington v. Heckel 137
Watkins v. Conway 110
Watson v. Employers Liability Assurance Corp. 63
Wells v. Simonds Abrasive Co. 69
White v. Tenant 9
Wilmington Trust Co. v. Wilmington Trust Co. 19
World-Wide Volkswagen Corp. v. Woodson 84

Y

Yarborough v. Yarborough 115
Yunis, United States v. 123

ALABAMA GREAT SOUTHERN RAILROAD v. CARROLL

Ala. Sup. Ct., 97 Ala. 126, 11 So. 803 (1892).

NATURE OF CASE: Appeal in action seeking damages for negligence.

FACT SUMMARY: Carroll (P), an Alabama citizen, sought statutory remedies against an Alabama corporation for an extraterritorial tort.

CONCISE RULE OF LAW: Statutory remedies may not be pursued in courts of the state having such remedies when the cause of action arises in another state.

FACTS: Carroll (P) was an employee of Alabama Great Southern Railroad, Inc. (D). Both were Alabama citizens. Carroll (P), who was injured due to a car decoupling that occurred in Mississippi, brought a personal injury action in Alabama state court, seeking damages under common law tort theories, as well as Alabama's Employers' Liability Act. The Railroad (D) contended that the Act did not apply. [The casebook opinion did not state the result in the trial court. The Alabama Supreme Court, on appeal, dismissed the applicability of the Act.]

ISSUE: May statutory remedies be pursued in courts of the state having such remedies when the cause of action arises in another state?

HOLDING AND DECISION: (McClellan, J.) No. Statutory remedies may not be pursued in courts of the state having such remedies when the cause of action arises in another state. Whether a cause of action exists must be determined by the law prevailing at the time and place of the facts creating the cause of action. When a cause of action arises it may be enforced in any court having personal jurisdiction; however, the cause of action itself is a creature of the jurisdiction where the operative facts occurred. Here, the fact that both parties were Alabama citizens allowed an action to be maintained in Alabama courts, but did not justify recourse to Alabama law, nor to any implication that such law became part of Carroll's (P) employment contract. Therefore, no cause of action under the Employers' Liability Act can be maintained. [The casebook opinion did not state whether the trial court was reversed or affirmed.]

EDITOR'S ANALYSIS: The present case is an example of the traditional approach to conflicts of law in tort actions. To a large extent, it remains the approach most often utilized. However, courts today are much more likely to refer to local law if an identifiable forum-state interest exists.

[For more information on choice of law, see Casenote Law Outline on Conflict of Laws, Chapter 1, § III, Choice of Law.]

NOTES:

MARRA v. BUSHEE

317 F. Supp. 972 (D. Vt. 1970).

NATURE OF CASE: Motion for judgment n.o.v. upon award of damages for alienation of affection.

FACT SUMMARY: Marra (P), a New York resident, sued Bushee (D), a Vermont resident, for alienation of affection after her husband began cohabiting with her.

CONCISE RULE OF LAW: In an action based on alienation of affection, the law of the state where the alienating conduct occurred will control.

FACTS: Marra (P) and her husband lived in New York. The husband left Marra (P) and began cohabiting with Bushee (D) in Vermont. Under Vermont law, Marra (P) brought an alienation of affection action in U.S. district court in Vermont. A jury awarded her $9,000. Bushee (D) moved for judgment notwithstanding the verdict, contending that the court should have applied the law of New York, under which that cause of action had been abolished.

ISSUE: In an action based on alienation of affection, will the law of the state where the alienating conduct occurred control?

HOLDING AND DECISION: (Leddy, C.J.) Yes. In an action based on alienation of affection, the law of the state where the alienating conduct occurred will control. The traditional test for conflicts of laws in tort actions is that the law of the state where the tort occurred will control. When the tort is of the negligence variety, the rule is that the tort will be considered to have occurred where the harm is felt. However, when the nature of the tort is that of an intentional type, the place where the tortious conduct occurred will be considered to be where the tort occurred. Here, the conduct constituting the tort occurred in Vermont, and thus Vermont's law was applicable. As an incidental matter, even if the above rule is not given adherence, the same result would occur because, in an action of this type, affection/consortium is considered to follow the alienated spouse, not the plaintiff. Motion denied.

EDITOR'S ANALYSIS: The alienation of affection cause of action is largely a relic of a bygone era, and most states no longer recognize it. However, the present action has value in illustrating the approach to use in other, more relevant causes of action. Such actions can include assault and battery and defamation. Also, from a legal strategy standpoint, this case illustrates the advantages of utilizing diversity jurisdiction to achieve recovery from injury recognized in some states and not in others.

[For more information on conflicts and tort law, see Casenote Law Outline on Conflict of Laws, Chapter 6, § I, The Traditional Method.]

NOTES:

POOLE v. PERKINS
Va. Sup. Ct., 126 Va. 33, 101 S.E. 240 (1919).

NATURE OF CASE: Appeal of award of damages for breach of promissory note.

FACT SUMMARY: Poole (D), who had signed in Tennessee a promissory note payable in Virginia, raised an incapacity defense available in Tennessee but not Virginia.

CONCISE RULE OF LAW: When a contract is entered into in one state but is to be performed in another, the incapacity rules of the state of performance control.

FACTS: Poole (D) signed a promissory note in favor of Perkins (P) in the state of Tennessee. The note was payable in Virginia. Poole (D) defaulted, and Perkins (P) brought a collection action. Poole (D) raised the common law incapacity defense of coverture, which was available in Tennessee but not Virginia. The trial court, applying Virginia law, enforced the note, and Poole (D) appealed.

ISSUE: When a contract is entered into in one state but is to be performed in another, will the incapacity rules of the state of performance control?

HOLDING AND DECISION: (Kelly, J.) Yes. When a contract is entered into in one state but is to be performed in another, the incapacity rules of the state of performance control. The general rule is that the law of a contract's performance, not execution, will be applied in an action based upon the note. However, some have argued that when the issue is whether a contract has been formed, the law of the state of formation should apply. Incapacity is one such issue. This court is inclined to reject this argument. When parties make contracts which upon their face are to be discharged in a state other than that in which they are executed, it is presumed that they intended the law of the state of performance to apply. This is true with respect to all aspects of the contract, including formation. As contract construction strives to give effect to the parties' intentions, any contrary rule would be improper. Here, the parties specified performance in Virginia, so Virginia law applied. Affirmed.

EDITOR'S ANALYSIS: Coverture was an early common law concept relating to married women. Based on the concept of a marital household being "one flesh," a married woman could not contract in her own right. This doctrine has long been rejected. However, the present opinion remains illustrative of conflicts of law with respect to incapacity in general.

[For more information on conflicts and contract law, see Casenote Law Outline on Conflict of Laws, Chapter 7, § I, The Traditional Approaches.]

NOTES:

LINN v. EMPLOYERS REINSURANCE CORP.
Pa. Sup. Ct., 392 Pa. 58, 159 A.2d 638 (1958).

NATURE OF CASE: Appeal of nonsuit in action for damages for breach of contract.

FACT SUMMARY: A commission contract between Linn (P) and Employers Reinsurance Corp. (D) involved offers and acceptances made in different states.

CONCISE RULE OF LAW: When a contract offer and acceptance are made telephonically in different states, the law of the state where acceptance is made controls with respect to contractual validity.

FACTS: Linn (P) and other Pennsylvania-based insurance brokers offered one Ehmann, agent of Employers Reinsurance Corp. (D), to perform certain services which would bring new accounts to Employers (D), in exchange for 5% commissions. Ehmann relayed the deal to Employers' (D) home office, and the decision was made to accept. Ehmann telephonically informed Linn (P) that the offer had been accepted. Years later, Employers (D) reneged, and Linn (P) and others sued for breach. Employers (D) raised New York's statute of frauds. The trial court, accepting New York law, granted a nonsuit. An appeal followed.

ISSUE: When a contract offer and acceptance are made telephonically in different states, will the law of the state where acceptance is made control with respect to contractual validity?

HOLDING AND DECISION: (Cohen, J.) Yes. When a contract offer and acceptance are made telephonically in different states, the law of the state where acceptance is made controls with respect to contractual validity. The validity of a contract is determined by reference to the law of the place of contracting. In the case of acceptance of an offer by mail or telegraph, the place of contracting has traditionally been where the offeree or agent thereof sends the message of acceptance. The same rule should be applied to telephonic offer-acceptances. Consequently, the law of the state where Ehmann placed his call to Linn (P) should control. Since the record is unclear as to where this place was, the matter must be remanded for a determination of this location. Reversed and remanded.

EDITOR'S ANALYSIS: The choice of law employed by the court here should be contrasted with the traditional conflicts rule for tort cases. Under the tort approach, the law of the place where the cause of action arose usually controls. Under the contracts analysis employed in the case above, the place where the cause of action arose is irrelevant to determining which jurisdiction's law should apply.

[For more information on offer and acceptance, see Casenote Law Outline on Conflict of Laws, Chapter 7, § I, The Traditional Approaches.]

NOTES:

WHITE v. TENANT
31 W.Va. 790, 8 S.E. 596 (1888).

NATURE OF CASE: Appeal of dismissal of action to set aside the settlement and distribution of a decedent's estate according to West Virginia law.

FACT SUMMARY: White (P) sued Tenant (D), who was the administrator of a decedent's estate, to have the estate settled according to Pennsylvania law and not West Virginia law.

CONCISE RULE OF LAW: The law of the state in which a decedent had his domicile when he died will control the distribution of his personal estate. Domicile is an actual or inchoate residence with no intention to make a domicile elsewhere.

FACTS: The decedent had life-long domicile in West Virginia. He sold his property in West Virginia and left for Pennsylvania the same evening, with the intention of making Pennsylvania his home. The decedent and his wife arrived in Pennsylvania, unpacked, but returned to West Virginia that night because the house was cold and damp and the wife was not feeling well. The decedent cared for his wife daily but returned daily to Pennsylvania to look after his home there. The decedent died in West Virginia shortly thereafter. The estate was subsequently administered per West Virginia law which was more favorable to his wife than Pennsylvania law. The siblings of the decedent (P) sued the administrator (D) to have the will settled according to Pennsylvania law which would be more favorable to them. The circuit court dismissed the action of decedent's siblings (P), and they appealed.

ISSUE: At the time of the decedent's death, was his legal domicile in West Virginia or Pennsylvania?

HOLDING AND DECISION: (Snyder, J.)At the time of his death, decedent's domicile was Pennsylvania. By leaving a former domicile without any intention of returning, and by moving into a new domicile with the intention of staying indefinitely, the domicile has changed. It doesn't matter how long one actually stays in the new domicile, so long as the purpose of establishing a new domicile doesn't change. The decedent in this case abandoned his residence in West Virginia with the intention and purpose of not returning and of making his home in Pennsylvania for an indefinite time. This intention was proven based on circumstances, the decedent's declarations, and his acts. It was impossible for him to return to his West Virginia home because it had been sold. The house he rented in Pennsylvania had no use except to be lived in. Household goods and stock had been moved. It was only after he had arrived in Pennsylvania that he failed to remain there. He had no change in his purpose of making Pennsylvania his home. It was, therefore, Pennsylvania law which controlled, because Pennsylvania was the decedent's domicile, notwithstanding that he died in West Virginia. Reversed.

EDITOR'S ANALYSIS: If domicile once existed, be it by one day of residence or by abandonment of the old domicile and being en route to the new, that domicile is sufficient for new domicile existence. Mere temporary absence will not destroy the new domicile, no matter how long the absence. The intention not to return to the old domicile controls. Furthermore, domicile continues until it is changed for another. One can only have one domicile at a time.

RODRIGUEZ DIAZ v. SIERRA MARTINEZ
853 F.2d 1027 (1st Cir. 1988).

NATURE OF CASE: Appeal of dismissal of personal injury action.

FACT SUMMARY: Diaz (P) claimed to be a citizen of New York even though he had been a domiciliary of Puerto Rico and was still a minor under Puerto Rico law.

CONCISE RULE OF LAW: A person may change his domicile to another state even if, under the law of the former domicile, he is incompetent to do so.

FACTS: Rodriguez Diaz (P) lived in Puerto Rico. At age 17, he was involved in a motor vehicle accident. He subsequently moved to New York. He later filed a personal injury action against the other driver, Sierra Martinez (D) and a medical facility in U.S. District Court in Puerto Rico. At the time he filed the action, he was 18. Puerto Rico's age of adulthood was 21, while New York's was 18. The district court dismissed for want of diversity, holding that since Diaz (P) was a minor under Puerto Rico law he was incompetent to change his domicile and thus remained a Puerto Rican domiciliary. Diaz (P) appealed.

ISSUE: May a person change his domicile to another state even if, under the law of the former domicile, he is incompetent to do so?

HOLDING AND DECISION: (Campbell, C.J.) Yes. A person may change his domicile to another state even if, under the law of the former domicile, he is incompetent to do so. The state of a person's citizenship/domicile, for purposes of diversity jurisdiction in federal court, is not determined by state law but rather by federal common law. This court believes that the purposes of diversity jurisdiction are best met by reference to the domiciliary laws of the state in which a litigant is physically present. Any other source of law with respect to domicile requirements could lead to the anomalous situation of a person being domiciliary of the state of residence in some suits and not in others. Consequently, to promote uniformity in the federal judiciary, whether a person is a domiciliary of a state is to be determined by the law of that person's residence. Here, the district court erroneously applied Puerto Rico law. Reversed.

DISSENT: (Torvella, J.) The issue of change of domicile's one of capacity, not intention, and Diaz (P) was incapable of so changing.

EDITOR'S ANALYSIS: Domicile is a matter of both objective and subjective factors. Objectively, physical presence is required, although it is not required at all times. Subjectively, an intent to return or remain is needed. Intent can be proved by both direct and circumstantial evidence.

[For more information on ascertaining a person's domicile, see Casenote Law Outline on Conflict of Laws, Chapter 5, § V, Ascertaining a Person's Domicile.]

NOTES:

IN RE MAY'S ESTATE
N.Y. Ct. App., 305 N.Y. 486, 114 N.E.2d 4 (1953).

NATURE OF CASE: Appeal of order reversing appointment of estate administrator.

FACT SUMMARY: The appointment of Sam May as administrator for the estate of his late wife was challenged on the basis that the marriage, legal in the state of its solemnization, was illegal in New York, where they resided.

CONCISE RULE OF LAW: A marriage valid in the state of its solemnization will be considered legal in New York.

FACTS: Sam and Fannie May were married in Rhode Island in 1913. They were uncle and niece by half-blood. Rhode Island permitted such marriages by persons of Jewish faith, which the Mays were. The Mays moved to New York, where they lived until Fannie's death in 1945. In 1951, Alice Greenberg, a daughter of the Mays, petitioned to be appointed administrator of Fannie's estate. Sam objected, contending that he, as surviving spouse, was entitled to continue in that role. Greenberg contended that, because an uncle-niece marriage was void in New York, Sam was not a surviving spouse. The trial court agreed and granted the petition. The appellate division reversed, and the New York Court of Appeals granted review.

ISSUE: Will a marriage valid in the state of its solemnization be considered legal in New York?

HOLDING AND DECISION: (Lewis, C.J.) Yes. A marriage valid in the state of its solemnization will be considered legal in New York. New York's law regarding incestuous marriage does not by its terms purport to have extraterritorial effect. This being so, such language should not be read into the statute. Consequently, a marriage valid under the law of its creation will not be invalidated by virtue of the fact that it would be considered incestuous and therefore invalid under New York law. This was the position of the appellate division. Affirmed.

DISSENT: (Desmond, J.) The Mays were New York citizens who went to Rhode Island specifically to take advantage of its marriage laws. New York law should have extraterritorial application to its citizens even when they are out of the jurisdiction.

EDITOR'S ANALYSIS: Marriage and divorce is a field of law left almost entirely to the states, with little federal intervention. Because of this, conflict of law issues frequently arise. Probably the most common conflict situation has been the "quickie" divorce situation, although modern no-fault divorce laws have lessened the frequency of such proceedings.

[For more information on marriage validity, see Casenote Law Outline on Conflict of Laws, Chapter 10, § II, Determinations of Invalidity of Marriage.]

NOTES:

LANHAM v. LANHAM

Wis. Sup. Ct., 136 Wis. 360, 117 N.W. 787 (1908).

NATURE OF CASE: Appeal of grant of petition for support out of a decedent's estate.

FACT SUMMARY: Lanham (P), putative surviving spouse of a decedent, had married the decedent in Michigan, less than one year after her divorce, to evade Wisconsin's prohibition against a divorcee's remarriage within one year of the divorce.

CONCISE RULE OF LAW: Wisconsin's law forbidding marriages within one year of a divorcee's divorce has extraterritorial application.

FACTS: Sarah Lanham (P) divorced her first husband and soon thereafter married James Lanham. Both Lanhams were Wisconsin citizens. They married in Michigan. Upon James' death, Sarah (P) petitioned for support from James' estate as surviving spouse. The heirs of James opposed the petition, contending that the marriage was void due to Wisconsin's law prohibiting remarriages by a divorcee within one year of divorce.

ISSUE: Does Wisconsin's law forbidding marriages within one year of a divorcee's divorce have extraterritorial application?

HOLDING AND DECISION: (Winslow, C.J.) Yes. Wisconsin's law forbidding marriages within one year of a divorcee's divorce has extraterritorial application. Generally speaking, marriages valid in the state of celebration are valid in Wisconsin even if they would not be valid if solemnized in Wisconsin. However, when such marriage violates a public policy as expressed by a law, such law will have extraterritorial effect. In this instance, the purpose of the law is to discourage the use of divorce as a means of leaving a spouse to remarry and, thus, was enacted to promote family stability, an important goal. To allow Wisconsin citizens to evade this law by marrying elsewhere would eviscerate it, so it should be given extraterritorial effect. Here, the Lanhams' marriage was invalid under Wisconsin law and was void ab initio. Reversed.

EDITOR'S ANALYSIS: Issues of marriage validity usually arise in a divorce or probate situation. Consequently, the intent of the parties in marrying where they did is often difficult to ascertain. Some states make such intent a factor in the validity analysis. Most do not.

[For more information on divorce, see Casenote Law Outline on Conflict of Laws, Chapter 10, § III, Termination or Dissolution of Marriage by Divorce.]

NOTES:

BURR v. BECKLER

Ill. Sup. Ct., 264 Ill. 230, 106 N.E. 206 (1914).

NATURE OF CASE: Appeal of reinstatement of action seeking foreclosure sale.

FACT SUMMARY: Beckler (D) pledged certain Illinois real estate as collateral for a note executed in Florida.

CONCISE RULE OF LAW: An instrument affecting title to Illinois real estate will not be valid if, under the law of the place it was executed, the instrument was void.

FACTS: Beckler (D), a married woman, pledged as collateral for a promissory note certain real estate in Chicago that she owned. She executed the note and trust deed in Florida and mailed them to Burr's (P) assignor. Beckler (D) eventually defaulted on the note, and Burr (P), who had been assigned the note, instituted a foreclosure action. Beckler (D) raised the Florida defense of coverture, arguing that she had been incompetent to execute the note. The trial court agreed and dismissed the action. The court of appeals reversed, and Beckler (D) appealed.

ISSUE: Will an instrument affecting title to Illinois real estate be valid if, under the law of the place it was executed, it was void?

HOLDING AND DECISION: (Cartwright, C.J.) No. An instrument affecting title to Illinois real estate will not be valid if, under the law of the place it was executed, the instrument was void. As a general rule, instruments affecting title to real estate will be judged with reference to the law of the place where the property is situated. The exception to this relates to formation of the instrument. Whether the instrument was in fact formed is determined by the law of the place of formation. Here, the instruments in question were delivered by Beckler (D) in Florida, so Florida law controls. Because, under Florida law, Beckler (D) was incompetent to contract under its coverture law, the instruments were void. Reversed.

EDITOR'S ANALYSIS: The rule regarding formation is only an exception to the general rule that situs state law affects real property. Various reasons exist for the general rule. For one, title records are kept in states regarding only that property within its jurisdiction. Another oft-cited reason is that the situs state has ultimate control over that property.

[For more information on real estate, see Casenote Law Outline on Conflict of Laws, Chapter 8, § I, Land.]

NOTES:

THOMPSON v. KYLE

Fla. Sup. Ct., 39 Fla. 582, 23 So. 12 (1897).

NATURE OF CASE: Appeal of order foreclosing a mortgage.

FACT SUMMARY: Thompson (D) mortgaged her Alabama real estate to secure a debt of her husband, an act that was valid in Florida but void in Alabama, the state where the transaction occurred.

CONCISE RULE OF LAW: An otherwise valid encumbrance upon real estate will not be void on account of incapacity laws in the mortgagor's domiciliary state.

FACTS: Thompson (D), an Alabama resident, mortgaged certain Florida real estate to secure a debt incurred by her husband. The transactions were executed in Alabama. Such an encumbrance was valid under Florida law but void under Alabama law. Kyle (P), the creditor, later brought a foreclosure action. Thompson (D) contended that Alabama law should be applied, and that the mortgage was therefore invalid. The trial court foreclosed the mortgage, and Thompson (D) appealed.

ISSUE: Will an otherwise valid encumbrance upon real estate be void on account of incapacity laws in the mortgagor's domiciliary state?

HOLDING AND DECISION: (Carter, J.) No. An otherwise valid encumbrance upon real estate will not be void on account of incapacity laws in the mortgagor's domiciliary state. Transactions affecting title to real property are to be regulated with reference to the law of the state within which the property is situated. Realty within a jurisdiction is subject to the law of that jurisdiction, and parties executing instruments affecting title thereto are presumed to refer to the law of that jurisdiction. Here, despite the fact that the parties are Alabama domiciliaries and the instrument of encumbrance was executed in Alabama, the law of Florida should apply because that is where the property is situated. Affirmed.

EDITOR'S ANALYSIS: The opinion states that extraterritorial parties are "presumed" to contract with respect to the law of the jurisdiction containing the property. The question presents itself as to whether this presumption can be rebutted. The opinion is silent on this issue, but it seems that the thrust of the opinion is that the law of the controlling jurisdiction will always apply.

[For more information on real estate, see Casenote Law Outline on Conflict of Laws, Chapter 8, § I, Land.]

NOTES:

VANDERPOEL v. GORMAN
140 N.Y. 563, 35 N.E. 932 (1894).

NATURE OF CASE: Appeal of order dismissing action to release lien on real property.

FACT SUMMARY: A New Jersey corporation, doing business in New York, made certain assignments of New York situated property for the benefit of creditors, including Vanderpoel (P), an act legal in New Jersey but not in New York.

CONCISE RULE OF LAW: A foreign corporation may make assignments of property which are legal in the state of incorporation, even when illegal in the state where the property is located.

FACTS: North River Lumber Company was a New Jersey corporation licensed to do business in New York. Approaching insolvency, it made a general assignment of its property to Vanderpoel (P), assignee of selected creditors. General assignments were legal in New Jersey but not in New York. Certain creditors not favored by the assignment commenced execution of property situated in New York. Gorman (D), a sheriff, levied execution. Vanderpoel (P) commenced an action to release the lien placed on the property due to the levy of execution. The trial court held the assignment invalid, and Vanderpoel (P) appealed.

ISSUE: May a foreign corporation make assignments of property which are legal in the state of incorporation, but illegal in the state where the property is located?

HOLDING AND DECISION: (Peckham, J.) Yes. A foreign corporation may make assignments of property which are legal in the state of incorporation, even if local law prohibits such assignments. New York law prohibits corporations from making such assignments. However, the language of the law does not purport to cover foreign corporations. This being so, the proper reading of the statute is that the Legislature intended it to apply to domestic corporations only. Corporations are creatures of the law of the state of incorporation, and its affairs are to be governed by the laws of the incorporating state. This court will not read into New York's law regarding assignments the extraordinary aspect of having an effect on foreign corporations. Since as a general rule corporations can make general assignments, and New York's law does not apply to foreign corporations, Vanderpoel (P) received a valid assignment. Reversed.

EDITOR'S ANALYSIS: The present case was more a matter of statutory construction than one of a state's power over foreign corporations. The New York Court of Appeals apparently conceded that New York's legislature could have prohibited foreign corporation assignments if it had so desired. The concept appearing strange to the court, it declined to give extraterritorial effect to the law absent express language to that effect.

[For more information on transfers of title, see Casenote Law Outline on Conflict of Laws, Chapter 8, § II, Personalty.]

NOTES:

IRVING TRUST CO. v. MARYLAND CASUALTY CO.
83 F.2d 168 (2d Cir. 1936).

NATURE OF CASE: Appeal of dismissal of action to compel conveyance of real and personal property.

FACT SUMMARY: A bankruptcy trustee attempted, in a New York court, to void a preferential transfer by a foreign bankrupt located in New York, an act legal in the state of incorporation.

CONCISE RULE OF LAW: A preferential transfer by a foreign bankrupt doing business in New York is not void if allowed under local law.

FACTS: The Irving Trust Co. (P) was named trustee of an involuntary bankrupt, which was located in New York. The bankrupt had, prior to the petition, made certain preferential transfers to creditors. The bankrupt was a Delaware corporation licensed to do business in New York. Irving Trust (P) filed a bill in equity, seeking to void the transfer as bring unlawful under New York law. The transferred property was located in Delaware, where such transfer was lawful. The district court held Delaware law to apply and dismissed. Irving Trust (P) appealed.

ISSUE: Is a preferential transfer by a foreign bankrupt doing business in New York void if allowed under local law?

HOLDING AND DECISION: (Hand, J.) No. A preferential transfer by a foreign bankrupt doing business in New York is not void if allowed under local law. Section 114 of New York's corporation law imposes liability on corporate directors or officers who make unlawful transfers of corporate property. Section 114 by its terms applies to corporation. However, § 114 does not purport to make those transfers void to themselves. Indeed, it could not do so, because the law of the place where the property is situated controls in such a situation. Here, the preferentially transferred property was situated in Delaware, so § 114 could not affect title to the property. (The court went on to hold that the district court could, however, use its equitable powers in personam to compel the bankrupt's officers or assignees thereof to reconvey the property, and on that basis reversed.)

EDITOR'S ANALYSIS: Preferential transfers have long been a problem with insolvent corporations. A company seeing bankruptcy on the horizon would often convey property to a favorite creditor, often a related concern, to the detriment of other creditors. In the past, the patchwork of state laws often facilitated such activities. Today, federal bankruptcy law makes such transfers voidable.

[For more information on transfers of title, see Casenote Law Outline on Conflict of Law, Chapter 8, § II, Personalty.]

NOTES:

McDERMOTT INC. v. LEWIS
531 A.2d 206 (Del. 1987).

NATURE OF CASE: Appeal of judgment voiding corporate reorganization.

FACT SUMMARY: McDermott, Inc. (P), a Delaware subsidiary of McDermott International, Inc., a Panama corporation, was reorganized to have voting shares of its parent, an arrangement legal in Panama but not in Delaware.

CONCISE RULE OF LAW: A foreign corporation may allow a subsidiary to own voting shares of its stock if local law so allows.

FACTS: McDermott International, Inc. was a Panama Corporation doing business in Louisiana. McDermott, Inc. (D) was a Delaware corporation, a non-wholly-owned subsidiary of International. A reorganization between the two corporations was effected wherein International became a 92% owner of McDermott, Inc. (D), and the latter became owner of 10% of International's voting stock. This resulted in International functionally owning its own voting stock, a practice illegal in Delaware but legal in Panama. Lewis (P), a minority shareholder of McDermott, Inc. (D) challenged the reorganization. The Chancery Court held that McDermott, Inc. (D) could not vote its shares in International's elections. McDermott, Inc. (D) appealed.

ISSUE: May a foreign corporation allow a subsidiary to own voting shares of its stock if local law so allows?

HOLDING AND DECISION: (Moore, J.) Yes. A foreign corporation may allow a subsidiary to own voting shares of its stock if local law so allows. It is a near-universal rule that the internal affairs of a corporation are to be regulated with reference to the law of the place of incorporation. The reasons for this are manifest. The internal affairs of a corporation require a single, constant, and equal law to avoid corporate fragmentation. To apply local law to a foreign corporation in matters regarding internal corporate policy simply because a corporation is amenable to service of process would produce intolerable confusion and inequalities within the corporation. For these reasons, the law of the place of incorporation must be followed with respect to internal corporate affairs. Here, as voting is such an affair, Panama law should have been followed. Reversed.

EDITOR'S ANALYSIS: In many areas the territoriality approach with respect to application of law has been jettisoned or, at least, modified. Respecting internal corporate affairs, however, such is not the case. Almost all states follow this rule strictly. The one notable exception is California, which has imposed its cumulative voting requirements on foreign corporations doing business there.

[For more information on transfers of title, see Casenote Law Outline on Conflict of Laws, Chapter 8, § II, Personalty.]

NOTES:

HUTCHINSON v. ROSS
N.Y. Ct. App., 262 N.Y. 381, 187 N.E. 65 (1933).

NATURE OF CASE: Appeal from reversal of order invalidating an inter vivos trust.

FACT SUMMARY: An inter vivos trust created by Ross' (D) late husband was invalid under the law of his state of domicile but valid under the law of the state where the trust corpus was located.

CONCISE RULE OF LAW: An inter vivos trust consisting of money accounts is valid if permitted under the law of the state where the accounts are located, even if the trust is invalid under the law of the settlor's domicile.

FACTS: Ross' (D) late husband executed a prenuptial agreement wherein he created a $125,000 trust in favor of his then wife-to-be and any children they might have. Ross (D) and her husband were citizens of Quebec. After the husband's father died and left a large legacy to him, he modified the original trust by enlarging it to $1 million, the corpus consisting of New York deposit accounts. Under Quebec law, a prenuptial agreement could not be changed even with the parties' consent. Such modification was allowed under the New York law. Ross' (D) husband lost his entire fortune in bad investments. Insolvent, he attempted to revoke the trust so that its corpus could be used to satisfy creditors, and he filed an action in New York state court to effect such revocation. He was put into involuntary bankruptcy, and Hutchinson (P) was appointed trustee. Hutchinson (P) successfully brought suit to invalidate the trust, but the appellate division reversed. The N.Y. Court of Appeals granted review.

ISSUE: Is an inter vivos trust consisting of money accounts valid if permitted under the law of the state where the accounts are located, even if the trust is invalid under the law of the settlor's domicile?

HOLDING AND DECISION: (Lehman, J.) Yes. An inter vivos trust consisting of money accounts is valid if permitted under the law of the state where they are located, even if the trust is invalid under the law of the settlor's domicile. The general rule is that, where chattels are concerned, the law of the place where they are located controls their disposition. This rule is based on the notion that since such property is protected by the jurisdiction where they are located, that jurisdiction's law should apply to them. The rule is also based on a desire to promote uniformity and predictability regarding their disposition. While money is not chattel, the same policy considerations apply, and the rule should be expanded to include deposit accounts. The fact that such accounts may be conveyed by inter vivos trust does not change this result. The fact that a inter vivos trust is merely one form of inter vivos conveyance does not alter the considerations enumerated above. Here, the modification of the prenuptial agreement, despite its invalidity in Quebec, would be valid in New York. Since the deposit accounts were in New York, the modification was valid. Affirmed.

EDITOR'S ANALYSIS: Trusts can be created either inter vivos or by will. Generally speaking, courts defer, in will situations, to the law of the testator's domicile. Had the trust in this case been of the testamentary variety, the result would most likely have been different.

[For more information on trusts and conflicts, see Casenote Law Outline on Conflict of Laws, Chapter 8, § III, Trusts.]

NOTES:

WILMINGTON TRUST CO. v. WILMINGTON TRUST CO.
Del. Sup. Ct., 26 Del. Ch. 397, 24 A.2d 309 (1942).

NATURE OF CASE: Appeal of order validating provisions of a trust instrument.

FACT SUMMARY: The domicile of a testator of a testamentary trust was contended to be the situs of operative law governing the trust.

CONCISE RULE OF LAW: A trust is not necessarily governed by the law of the jurisdiction where the settlor/testator was domiciled.

FACTS: William Donner, a New York resident, created a testamentary trust naming his wife trustee and designating as beneficiaries various lineal descendants. The trust contained language to the effect that successor trustees could be appointed having the same powers as the original trustee. The Wilmington Trust Co. (D) was named successor trustee. Subsequent to this, Wilmington Trust (P), in its capacity as guardian of two of Donners' children, sued to invalidate portions of the trust which earmarked proceeds for other beneficiaries. The Chancellor, applying New York law, held that the trust violated New York's rule against perpetuities and prepared to invalidate the trust. The Chancellor then died, and his replacement, ruling that the law of Delaware, where the trust property was now located, applied, upheld the trust. Wilmington Trust (P) appealed.

ISSUE: Is a trust necessarily governed by the law of the jurisdiction where the settlor testator was domiciled?

HOLDING AND DECISION: (Layton, C.J.) No. A trust is not necessarily governed by the law of the jurisdiction where the settlor/testator was domiciled. Earlier cases have tended to focus on the domicile of the testator as the appropriate source of applicable law, and this remains a factor to be considered. However, courts should be primarily guided by the intent of the testator, as expressed by the terms of the instrument, as parties to such instruments are generally free to make such choices. Here, the instrument contained language allowing appointment of a new trustee, with such appointment having the effect of an initial appointment. The Chancellor construed this to mean that if such appointment involved a trustee in a different state, as this did, the new state became the state of the trust's creation. This was a legitimate construction. Affirmed.

EDITOR'S ANALYSIS: As a general rule, courts try to construe documents to effect the testator's intent. A construction according to New York law would have frustrated his intent. It is quite likely that to some extent this influenced the court's holding. This is often an unspoken factor in the construction of instruments.

[For more information on trusts, see Casenote Law Outline on Conflict of Laws, Chapter 8, § III, Trusts.]

NOTES:

19

MORSON v. SECOND NATIONAL BANK OF BOSTON

306 Mass. 588, 29 N.E.2d 19 (1940).

NATURE OF CASE: Appeal of order determining ownership of shares of stock.

FACT SUMMARY: A transfer of shares of stock of Massachusetts Mohair Plush Co. was done in accordance with the law of the state of incorporation but not of the state where the transfer physically occurred.

CONCISE RULE OF LAW: The effectiveness of a transfer of shares of stock shall be analyzed by reference to the law of the state of incorporation, not that of the situs of transfer.

FACTS: Turner owned shares of Massachusetts Mohair Plush Co., Inc. While in Italy, he attempted to effect, through endorsement of stock certificates, a transfer of his shares to Mildred Turner Coppermen. The endorsement procedure was valid under the law of Massachusetts, Mohair's state of incorporation, but arguably not under the law of Italy. After Turner's death, his administrator, Morson (P), sought to recover the stock on the basis of invalid transfer. (The casebook opinion did not cite the result in the trial court.)

ISSUE: Shall the effectiveness of a transfer of shares of stock be analyzed by reference to the law of the state of incorporation as opposed to that of the situs of transfer?

HOLDING AND DECISION: (Qua, J.) Yes. The effectiveness of a transfer of shares of stock shall be analyzed by reference to the law of the state of incorporation, not that of the situs of transfer. A distinction is to be made between shares of stock and the certificates embodying them. Shares are part of a corporate structure, and matters involving the internal structure of a corporation are to be governed by the law of the state of incorporation. The transfer of shares, therefore, should be referenced to the law of the place of incorporation, no matter where the physical transfer of certificates occurs. Here, the state of incorporation was Massachusetts, and its law applied to the transfer. Reversed.

EDITOR'S ANALYSIS: Transfers of chattel are generally governed by the law of the place of transfer. Stock in a corporation can be characterized as chattel. However, a transfer of stock, since it is an internal corporate matter, is considered to occur where the corporation is located, not where the stock certificates are located.

[For more information on transfer of personalty, see Casenote Law Outline on Conflict of Laws, Chapter 8, § II, Personalty.]

NOTES:

HAUMSCHILD v. CONTINENTAL CASUALTY CO.
Wis. Sup. Ct., 7 Wis.2d 130, 95 N.W.2d 814 (1959).

NATURE OF CASE: Suit in tort by wife against husband.

FACT SUMMARY: Mrs. Haumschild (P) was injured due to her husband's negligence while they were traveling in California. The couple was domiciled in Wisconsin where suit was brought.

CONCISE RULE OF LAW: Interspousal immunity for tort actions is a rule of family law and not of tort law, and the law of the spouses' domicile governs, not the law of the place of the wrong.

FACTS: Mrs. Haumschild (P) and her husband (D) were residents of Wisconsin but were traveling in California. While in California, Mrs. Haumschild (P) was injured due to her husband's (D) negligence in a car accident. California law prohibited a suit by a wife against her husband, or vice versa, for negligence. Wisconsin law contained no such prohibition. Suit was brought by Mrs. Haumschild (P) against her husband (D) in Wisconsin.

ISSUE: Where the place of the wrong prohibits interspousal suits for negligence, may the court of the spouses' domicile apply its own law which would allow such suits?

HOLDING AND DECISION: (Currie, J.) Yes. Where the place of the wrong prohibits interspousal suits for negligence, the court of the spouses' domicile may apply its own law which would allow such suits. The case presented is an issue of capacity to sue due to marital status. This relates to substantive family law and not to substantive tort law. While the majority of the states recognize the place of the wrong as governing capacity, we feel that the state of the domicile has a greater interest in such cases than the state where the wrong occurred. While California's conflict of laws rule would refer to our law to determine the wife's capacity, we do not feel it proper to resort to the awkward principles of renvoi to achieve what we feel to be the desired result. The law of the place of the wrong will govern as to substantive tort law, but the law of the domicile will govern as to capacity to sue. Mrs. Haumschild should be allowed to recover.

CONCURRENCE: (Fairchild, J.) Since the law of California would refer the issue back to Wisconsin law, I do not feel it necessary that this court take the position it has in regard to the substantive issues of tort and family law.

EDITOR'S ANALYSIS: If the state of domicile will govern on the issue of interspousal immunity, then a California wife injured by her husband would be denied recovery in a Wisconsin court. But if the state of domicile views the immunity question as procedural tort law, the court's decision would appear unsatisfactory. Wisconsin would then be imposing its substantive family law as a substitute for the other state's procedural tort law. On balance, however, the Wisconsin court's approach would appear to be well-reasoned, since the marital partners' expectations (in a fictional sense) would appear to be grounded in the family law of their domicile.

[For more information on substantive law, see Casenote Law Outline on Conflict of Laws, Chapter 5, § II, Classifying Rules as Substantive or Procedural.]

NOTES:

IN RE ESTATE OF DAMATO
N.J. Super. Ct., 86 N.J. Super. 107, 206 A.2d 171 (1965).

NATURE OF CASE: Appeal of probate court judgement adjudicating the rights to deposit accounts.

FACT SUMMARY: In a New Jersey probate action involving two Florida deposit accounts, it was urged that Florida conflict-of-law rules be applied.

CONCISE RULE OF LAW: In an action involving foreign deposit accounts, the foreign state's law of such accounts, but not its conflict-of-law rules, will be applied.

FACTS: When Damato, a New Jersey domiciliary, died, it was found that he had established two Florida deposit accounts. They had apparently been created "in trust" for his son, Philip. In a probate proceeding, James, Damato's other son, contended that the New Jersey court should apply Florida's conflicts law, which would result in application of New Jersey substantive law with respect to deposit accounts. The probate court elected to follow Florida substantive law, which resulted in the accounts going to Philip. James appealed.

ISSUE: In an action involving foreign deposit accounts, should the foreign state's law of conflicts be applied?

HOLDING AND DECISION: (LaBrecque, J.) No. In an action involving foreign deposit accounts, the foreign state's law of such accounts, but not its conflict-of-law rules, will be applied. The rule is that the disposition of deposit accounts will be governed by the substantive law of the location where the accounts are created. However, the conflicts-of-law rules of that state is not a body of substantive law to be applied by a forum state. Thus, a forum state should employ its own conflicts-of-law rules, which in this case means applying Florida substantive law with respect to the deposit accounts. Since under Florida law it appeared that the accounts were created for the benefit of Philip, the probate court was correct in awarding the account proceeds to him. Affirmed.

EDITOR'S ANALYSIS: The "trust" created for Philip is what is commonly known as a "Totten trust." This was named after the landmark New York case In re Totten, 179 N.Y. 112 (1904). A "Totten trust" is nothing more than a single bank account opened by one person in trust for another. Even though the party who opened the draft account can maintain control of the account funds during life, upon that party's death, the trust beneficiary takes the trust account proceeds, usually outside of probate.

[For more information on decedents' estates, see Casenote Law Outline on Conflict of Laws, Chapter 8, § IV, Wills and Inheritance; Decedent's Estates.]

NOTES:

UNIVERSITY OF CHICAGO v. DATER
Mich. Sup. Ct., 277 Mich. 653, 270 N.W. 175 (1936).

NATURE OF CASE: Appeal of denial of order to collect on a note.

FACT SUMMARY: Price (D) signed a note and mailed it to the lender while in Michigan.

CONCISE RULE OF LAW: The law applied in a debt collection action will be that of where it is mailed to the lender.

FACTS: Mr. and Mrs. Price (D) executed a promissory note in favor of the University of Chicago (P). The note and trust deed on certain collateralized real estate, located in Chicago, were signed in Michigan. The papers were then mailed in Michigan to the trust deed trustee. Mr. Price subsequently died, and, when the payments went into arrears, a collection action was filed. The trial court held Michigan law applicable, under which Price (D), as a married woman, had not had capacity to execute the note. A defense verdict was rendered as to her, and the University of Chicago (P) appealed.

ISSUE: Will the law applied in a debt collection action be that of where it is mailed to the lender?

HOLDING AND DECISION: (Wiest, J.) Yes. The law applied in a debt collection action will be that of where it is mailed to the lender. Generally speaking, when a contract does not by its terms designate the law to be applied, the law that shall be applied will be that of where the contract is to be performed. In the case of a promissory note, the place of delivery to the lender or trustee is where the contract is performed; that is when the contractual rights of the parties come into being. When the note is delivered via mail, delivery is deemed to be at the place of mailing, not the place of receipt. Here, the note was mailed in Michigan, so it was therefore delivered there. Consequently, Michigan law applies, and under Michigan law, Price (D) had been incompetent to incur the debt. Affirmed.

DISSENT: (Sharpe, J.) When a party in one state contracts with a party in another, and that party is competent to do so in only one of the states, it is presumed that the parties intended the law of the place where both parties are competent to apply.

DISSENT: (Butzel, J.) The notes were dated and payable in Illinois, which was also where the collateral was located. These facts make the place of contract Illinois.

EDITOR'S ANALYSIS: The issue here was dealt with in the Uniform Commercial Code. Article 9, the article dealing with security interests, states that the law of the place where the debtor is located will govern security interests. A debtor is "located" at his main (or sole) place of business.

[For more information on the law of the place of performance, see Casenote Law Outline on Conflict of Laws, Chapter 7, § I, The Traditional Approaches.]

NOTES:

SAMPSON v. CHANNELL
110 F.2d 754 (1st Cir.);
cert. denied, 310 U.S. 650 (1940).

NATURE OF CASE: Appeal of denial of damages for personal injury.

FACT SUMMARY: In a federal diversity action, the law of the forum state required that contributory negligence be proved by the defendant while the law of the injury site was the opposite.

CONCISE RULE OF LAW: A federal court sitting in diversity should follow state law regarding burden of proof.

FACTS: Sampson (P) was involved in an auto accident with Channell's (D) decedent. Sampson (P) brought suit federal district court in Massachusetts jurisdiction being based on diversity. The incident had occurred in Maine. In Massachusetts, a defendant had to prove contributory negligence; in Maine, a plaintiff had to disprove it. The district court applied Maine law, and the jury returned a defense verdict. Sampson (P) appealed.

ISSUE: Should a federal court sitting in diversity follow state law regarding burden of proof?

HOLDING AND DECISION: (Magruder, J.) Yes. A federal court sitting in diversity should follow state law regarding burden of proof. The Supreme Court has held that a federal court sitting in diversity must follow state substantive law. Whether a law is substantive or procedural turns on whether the outcome of a case is likely to be different depending on the law applied. Burden of proof can be determinative in a case, so a federal court should categorize it as substantive and apply state law. The question then becomes, what law is to be applied. The Massachusetts Supreme Judicial Court has held contrary to the rule applied here, that burden of proof is a procedural rule and that the law of the forum state, not that of the place of the tort, is to be applied. The court is free to make that conclusion. Consequently, the district court here should have applied the law of Massachusetts, not Maine, and the failure to do so was error. Reversed.

EDITOR'S ANALYSIS: The Supreme Court case alluded to in the opinion was Erie Railroad Co. v. Tompkins, 304 U.S. 64 (1938). This case set down the broad proposition that, in diversity cases, federal courts must apply state substantive law. The opinion did not precisely define what makes law substantive, or what law to apply. The federal judiciary has been grappling with these issues ever since.

_____

[For more information on state law in federal courts, see Casenote Law Outline on Conflict of Laws, Chapter 4, § I, The Erie Doctrine.]

NOTES:

O'LEARY v. ILLINOIS TERMINAL RAILROAD
299 S.W.2d 873 (Mo. 1957).

NATURE OF CASE: Appeal of award of damages for personal injury.

FACT SUMMARY: In a suit arising out of an Illinois accident, the court applied the local law that contributory negligence was an affirmative defense rather than Illinois' law that the lack thereof was an element of a plaintiff's cause of action.

CONCISE RULE OF LAW: When the law of the site of an accident is that the plaintiff's due care is an element of the negligence cause of action, that law should be applied by the forum state.

FACTS: O'Leary (P) was injured in an accident when an automobile in which she was a passenger was struck by a railway train in Illinois. She was a Missouri resident. She sued Illinois Terminal Railroad (D) in a Missouri court. In Missouri, the rule was that contributory negligence was an element of the plaintiff's cause of action. Finding this to be a rule of procedure, the trial court applied the Missouri rule. A jury awarded O'Leary (P) $7,000. The court of appeals affirmed and the state supreme court granted review.

ISSUE: When the law of the site of an accident is that the plaintiff's due care is an element of the negligence cause of action, should that law be applied in the forum state?

HOLDING AND DECISION: (Hollingsworth, J.) Yes. When the law of the site of an accident is that the plaintiff's due care is an element of the negligence cause of action, that law should be applied. As a general rule, the substantive law of the site where a cause of action arises is that which should be applied. Procedural local law may be applied. Substantive law may be distinguished from that of procedure in that the former relates to the rights and duties incorporated in the cause of action. When a plaintiff's due care is an element of the negligence cause of action, it necessarily falls within the definition of substantive law and should be applied by the forum court. Here, the trial court erroneously failed to do so. Reversed.

EDITOR'S ANALYSIS: "Substative" v. "procedural" as a dichotomy is easy to state in terms of choice of law. It can be much harder to apply. In terms of the issue here, the present case could legitimately be seen as involving a burden-of-proof issues. Most courts would consider this a procedural matter, as did the trial court here.

[For more information on substantive law, see Casenote Law Outline on Conflict of Laws, Chapter 5, § II, Classifying Rules as Substantive or Procedural.]

NOTES:

GRANT v. McAULIFFE

Cal. Sup. Ct., 41 Cal. 2d 859, 264 P.2d 944 (1953).

NATURE OF CASE: Appeal of dismissals of actions for damages for personal injury.

FACT SUMMARY: McAuliffe (D), administrator of alleged tortfeasor/decedent Pullen, contended that the law of the place of injury should apply as to the issue of survival of a tort action against a decedent.

CONCISE RULE OF LAW: On the issue of survival of a tort action against a decedent, the law of the forum applies.

FACTS: Grant (P) and Manchester (P), California residents, were in an auto accident with California resident Pullen, who died from his injuries. Grant (P) and Manchester (P) filed personal actions against McAuliffe (D), Pullen's administrator, in California state court. McAuliffe (D) moved to dismiss on the grounds that, under the law of the place of accident, Arizona, a personal injury action did not survive a defendant's death. The trial court, agreeing that Arizona law applied, dismissed. The court of appeal affirmed, and Grant (P) and Manchester (P) appealed to the California Supreme Court.

ISSUE: On the issue of survival of a tort action against a decedent, does the law of the forum apply?

HOLDING AND DECISION: (Traynor, J.) Yes. On the issue of survival of a tort action against a decedent, the law of the forum applies. Generally speaking, in a tort action substantive law of the place of injury will apply, but the procedural law of the forum will still be applied by the forum courts. Precedents regarding survival of actions uniformly address survival of plaintiffs' causes of action, so this court essentially writes on a clean slate with respect to the question at hand. Survival is not an element of a cause of action, but rather relates to enforcement of a cause of action. This sounds more like procedure than substance. Further, the issue relates to the responsibilities of the decedent's executor, a matter clearly governed by forum state procedure. For these reasons, the better rule is that forum law should apply to the issue of survival of a cause of action against a decedent. Reversed.

EDITOR'S ANALYSIS: As a general rule, foreign law will be applied by a forum state only if doing so does not conflict with an articulated policy of the forum state. Here, application of Arizona law would have left the injured parties without remedy. While the court did not cite the exception as a basis for its ruling, it is unlikely that it did not play a part in the result.

[For more information on torts and conflicts, see Casenote Law Outline on Conflict of Laws, Chapter 6, § I, The Traditional Method.]

NOTES:

DUKE v. HOUSEN
Wyo. Sup. Ct., 589 P.2d 334;
cert. denied, 444 U.S. 863 (1979).

NATURE OF CASE: Appeal of award of damages for personal injury.

FACT SUMMARY: In a personal injury action, Duke (D) contended that the statue of limitations of the place of injury should apply.

CONCISE RULE OF LAW: In a personal injury action the statute of limitations of the place of injury should apply.

FACTS: Housen (P) was introduced to Duke (D) in April 1970. During that month she followed him as he engaged in his occupation as a long-haul truck driver. They engaged in sexual intercourse numerous times in different states. During this period of time, Duke (D) was infected with gonorrhea, a condition for which he sought and received treatment. He later informed Housen (P) of this fact, and she sought treatment. However, by early 1973, she was suffering abdominal pain. Exploratory surgery in July 1973, revealed abdominal adhesions having formed due to secondary infections, a condition not likely to be alleviated medically. In April 1974, Housen (P) filed a personal injury action in Wyoming state court against Duke (D). Duke (D) raised a statute of limitations defense. The trial court held that under Wyoming law the statue began to run only upon discovery of the adhesions, and therefore rejected the defense. A jury returned a verdict of $1,300,000. Duke (D) appealed, arguing that the law of the state where the injury occurred, not Wyoming, should have applied.

ISSUE: In a personal injury action, should the statute of limitations of the place of injury apply?

HOLDING AND DECISION: (Raper, J.) Yes. In a personal injury action the statute of limitations of the place of injury should apply. Wyoming has enacted a "borrowing" statute, providing that the statute of limitations of the place of injury should apply. This law has done away with the sometimes confusing distinction that courts previously had to make regarding whether the statute of limitations was procedural or substantive. Now, in any tort case, the law of the place of injury will be adopted. [The court went on to hold the place of injury to have been New York, where the pair had had their last sexual encounter. As New York's statute was three years and did not have a "delayed discovery" provision, the court held that the action should have been dismissed.] Reversed.

CONCURRENCE: (Thomas, J.) Since Housen's (P) illness was identified in the District of Columbia, its statute should have been applied.

DISSENT: (McClintlock, J.) Since it cannot be determined where the injury occurred, there is no statute to be borrowed. Therefore, Wyoming's statute should have been applied.

EDITOR'S ANALYSIS: Most states have borrowing statutes. An attempt at uniformity has been made in that a uniform limitations act has been drafted by commentators. However, most states have not adopted this proposed legislation.

_____

[For more information on statutes of limitation, see Casenote Law Outline on Conflict of Laws, Chapter 5, § II, Classifying Rules as Substantive or Procedural.]

NOTES:

MARCHLIK v. CORONET INSURANCE CO.
Ill. Sup. Ct., 40 Ill. 2d 327, 239 N.E.2d 799 (1968).

NATURE OF CASE: Appeal of dismissal of personal injury complaint.

FACT SUMMARY: Marchlik (P), suing in Illinois for an accident occurring in Wisconsin, contended that Wisconsin law permitting a direct action against a tortfeasor's insurer should be applied.

CONCISE RULE OF LAW: The law of the place of accident allowing a direct action against a torfeasor's insurer is not to be applied in an Illinois lawsuit.

FACTS: Marchlik (P), a Wisconsin resident, was involved in an auto accident while riding as a passenger with one Tapio. The other vehicle was driven by one Trombley. Both Tapio and Trombley were insured by Illinois insurance companies, and their respective policies had been issued in that state. Marchlik (P) brought an action in Illinois state court, contending that Wisconsin's statute allowing a direct action against a torfeasor's insurer should be applied. The Illinois court disagreed and dismissed the action. Marchlik (P) appealed.

ISSUE: Is the law of the place of accident allowing a direct action against a tortfeasor's insurer to be applied in an Illinois court?

HOLDING AND DECISION: (House, J.) No. The law of the place of accident allowing a direct action against a tortfeasor's insurer is not to be applied in an Illinois lawsuit. Generally speaking, the substantive law of the site where a cause of action arises should be applied by a court in another jurisdiction, while that court should follow its own substantive law. Here, it seems clear that Wisconsin's direct action statute creates a substantive right of action. However, the general rule will not be applied when to do so would conflict with the public policy of the forum state. In Illinois, several sections of the insurance code prohibit direct actions against insurers, expressing a policy preference against such actions. Also, as Wisconsin lacks a guest statute, which Illinois has enacted, the possibility of a wave of Wisconsin-based actions in Illinois is present. For these reasons, application of the direct action statute is contrary to Illinois public policy. Affirmed.

CONCURRENCE: (Ward, J.) The action should have been dismissed on forum non conveniens grounds.

EDITOR'S ANALYSIS: The "guest statute" upon which the court partially based its opinion was once fairly prevalent across the country. Such statutes disallowed suits by injured passengers against host motorists. Most states no longer have such laws. They have either been repealed or have been found to violate equal protection.

[For more information on conflicts and torts, see Casenote Law Outline on Conflict of Laws, Chapter 6, § I, The Traditional Method.]

NOTES:

HOLZER v. DEUTSCHE REICHSBAHN-GESELLSCHAFT
N.Y. Ct. App., 277 N.Y. 474, 14 N.E.2d 798 (1938).

NATURE OF CASE: Appeal of order striking portions of an answer in action for damages for breach of contract.

FACT SUMMARY: Schenker & Co. (D) raised as a defense to a breach of contract action a law passed by the German government prohibiting the employment of Jews.

CONCISE RULE OF LAW: In an action based on breach of an employment contract it may be raised as a defense by the employer that such breach was mandated by law.

FACTS: Holzer (P), a Jewish German, contracted with Schenker & Co. (D), a German corporation, for a term of employment. Prior to expiration of the contract, the German government adopted a law prohibiting the employment of Jews in certain occupations, including that held by Holzer (P). Schenker (D) released Holzer (P), who sued for breach of contract. The trial court, on motion, struck Schenker's (D) defense based on the law promulgated by the German government. Schenker (D) appealed.

ISSUE: In an action based on breach of an employment contract, may it be raised as a defense by the employer that such breach was mandated by law?

HOLDING AND DECISION: (Per Curiam) Yes. In an action based on breach of an employment contract, it may be raised as a defense by the employer that such breach was mandated by law. The law of the country where a contract was made must be respected by courts of a forum state. When the law of the state of contract provides a defense to a breach of contract action, that law must be followed by the forum state. Here, the law of Germany not only permitted breach, but mandated it. Therefore, as a matter of law, the contract could not have been breached. Reversed. [The court remanded for a determination of whether the terms of the contract called for payment to Holzer (P) even if he did not perform his contracted-for services.]

EDITOR'S ANALYSIS: Courts today are less accepting of foreign law they find repugnant. When foreign law is contrary to public policy, courts are likely not to enforce them. A court today would almost certainly not apply any law like the one of issue here, although it might excuse a contractual performance under a force majeure theory, even though the effect of excuse would be similar to recognition of the repugnant foreign law. It is thus more likely that damages would be awarded.

[For more information on contracts and conflicts, see Casenote Law Outline on Conflict of Laws, Chapter 7, § I, The Traditional Approaches.]

NOTES:

PAPER PRODUCTS CO. v. DOGGRELL
Tenn. Sup. Ct., 195 Tenn. 581, 261 S.W.2d 127 (1953).

NATURE OF CASE: Appeal of order dismissing collection action.

FACT SUMMARY: Paper Products (P), in a suit filed in Tennessee, contended that the court should apply Arkansas law respecting shareholder liability for the debts of an Arkansas corporation.

CONCISE RULE OF LAW: Generally, shareholder liability for the debts of a corporation is to be determined by the law of the state of incorporation, except when contrary to the public policy of the forum state.

FACTS: Doggrell (D), Konz, (D), and Whitaker formed Forrest City Wood Products, Inc. under Arkansas law. Paper Products Co. (P) became a creditor thereof, relying on the credit worthiness of the corporation alone. Forrest City (D) eventually went bankrupt. It later appeared that Forrest City (D) had not met all technicalities of Arkansas incorporation law, although the incorporators had made a good faith effort to do so. Paper Products (P) filed a Tennessee state court action against Doggrell (D) and Konz (D), Tennessee residents, contending that they were not shielded from personal liability on account of the failure of Forrest City to properly incorporate. The trial court, declining to give effect to Arkansas law by which shareholders would be held liable for corporate debts, dismissed the complaint. Paper Products (P) appealed.

ISSUE: Will the law of the state of incorporation determine whether individual holders are liable for the debts of a corporation?

HOLDING AND DECISION: (Tomlinson, J.) Yes. Generally, the liability of a shareholder for the debts of a corporation is to be determined by the law of the state of incorporation. However, this will not be the case when enforcing such law within the forum state is contrary to the policy of the forum state. In Tennessee, the law clearly mandates limited liability for shareholders absent manifest prejudice upon a creditor if such limitation is effected. Here Paper Products (P) at no time relied on the personal credit worthiness of Forrest City's (D) shareholders; it only sought to take advantage of an error in forming a de jure corporation. This is contrary to Tennessee public policy. Affirmed.

EDITOR'S ANALYSIS: The court here found Arkansas' law to be "penal" in character and, hence, unworthy of application. As a general rule, penal laws of another state will not be borrowed as will civil laws. The reasoning for this distinction is unclear, but it is near-universally accepted.

[For more information on grounds for not exercising judicial jurisdiction, see Casenote Law Outline on Conflict of Laws, Chapter 2, § IV, Grounds for Not Exercising Jurisdiction.]

NOTES:

TIDEWATER OIL CO. v. WALLER
302 F.2d 638 (10th Cir. 1962).

NATURE OF CASE: Appeal of award of damages for personal injury.

FACT SUMMARY: An Oklahoma federal district court, not being informed of applicable law of Turkey, the place where an accident occurred, applied local law.

CONCISE RULE OF LAW: When a forum state cannot ascertain the law of the state whose law should be applied, it may apply local law.

FACTS: Waller (P) was injured while in Turkey. He was performing services for Tidewater Oil (D) pursuant to a contract between it and Waller's (P) main employer, Spartan Aircraft Co. Waller (P) filed a diversity action in Oklahoma district court. Both sides agreed that Turkish law applied, but such law was not presented to the court. The court instead applied Oklahoma law, and a jury awarded damages. Tidewater Oil (D) appealed.

ISSUE: When a forum state cannot ascertain the law of the state whose law should be applied, may it apply local law?

HOLDING AND DECISION: (Murrah, J.) Yes. When a forum state cannot ascertain the law of the state whose law should be applied, it may apply local law. Unless it can be shown that the legal system of the foreign state is so fundamentally different from that of the forum state that it is unlikely that the two states' laws would be similar on a given issue, a forum state may substitute its own law for that of the other state whose law should be applied. Here, Turkey is a civil law state as opposed to a common law state such as Oklahoma. Nonetheless, there is a rational basis for presuming that Turkish law would embody the near-universal recognition that a tortfeasor may be liable to those he injures. For these reasons, the district court was within its rights in applying Oklahoma law.

EDITOR'S ANALYSIS: The Federal Rules of Evidence provide for the incorporation of the law of a foreign nation. One wishing to assert such a law must give reasonable notice thereof. The court may accept any reasonable material tending to prove foreign law, including testimony. The court may admit or execute such evidence as it might any other item of evidence.

[For more information on ascertaining foreign law, see Casenote Law Outline on Conflict of Laws, Chapter 5, § I, Proving Foreign Law.]

NOTES:

31

BABCOCK v. JACKSON

N.Y. Ct. App., 12 N.Y.2d 473, 191 N.E.2d 279, (1963).

NATURE OF CASE: Appeal of dismissal of personal injury action.

FACT SUMMARY: In a personal injury action arising out of an accident involving New York citizens and occurring in Ontario, Canada, a trial court dismissed on the basis of Ontario's guest statute.

CONCISE RULE OF LAW: The guest statute of the site of accident will not be applied in an action between citizens of the forum state.

FACTS: Babcock (P) was a passenger in a vehicle driven by Jackson (D) in Ontario, Canada. Both lived in New York. While driving, Jackson (D) lost control of the vehicle, and a crash ensued. Babcock (P) sued Jackson (D) for personal injury in New York state court. The trial court sustained Jackson's (D) motion to dismiss, applying Ontario's "guest statute," which prohibited an action by a passenger against a driver. The appellate division affirmed, and the N.Y. Court of Appeals granted review.

ISSUE: Will the guest statute of the site of accident be applied in an action between citizens of the forum state?

HOLDING AND DECISION: (Fuld, J.) No. The guest statute of the site of accident will not be applied in an action between citizens of the forum state. The law of the place of accident does not invariably govern a personal injury action. When the forum state's interests are greater than those of the state of accident, this being gauged by the parties' relative contacts with the two states, forum law will be applied. Here, New York's interests are undeniably greater. Both parties live in New York and the accident's occurrence in Ontario was a matter of pure fortuity. The purpose of Ontario's guest statue was to prevent fraud against insurance companies through collusion. Here, no Canadian insurer is involved, and Ontario has no interest in protecting a non-Canadian carrier. Because New York's interest is much greater than that of Ontario, Ontario's guest statue is not to be applied. Reversed.

DISSENT: (Van Voorhis, J.) The concept of significant contacts for purposes of applicable law was created to deal with contract law, not tort law, to which it should not be extended.

EDITOR'S ANALYSIS: It seems that the court could have taken a somewhat more conservative approach than it did and reached the same result. Traditionally, a foreign state's law would not be applied if doing so would unduly offend the forum state's public policy. The court here could have applied this role to the present tort case. Instead, it elected to use the (then) avant-garde contacts approach of contracts cases.

[For more information on guest statutes, see Casenote Law Outline on Conflict of Laws, Chapter 6, § II, Modern Approaches.]

NOTES:

TOOKER v. LOPEZ

N.Y. Ct. App., 24 N.Y.2d 569, 249 N.E.2d 394, (1969).

NATURE OF CASE: Appeal of order striking affirmative defense in wrongful death action.

FACT SUMMARY: In an action concerning a Michigan accident involving two New York citizens and a New York-registered vehicle, a New York court declined to apply Michigan's guest statute.

CONCISE RULE OF LAW: In a personal injury action in which all the parties are forum state citizens, the guest statute of the jurisdiction of accident will not be applied.

FACTS: Catharina Tooker and Marcia Lopez were New York citizens rooming together at Michigan State University. While in a vehicle registered and insured in New York Lopez, the driver, lost control of the vehicle. The resultant accident killed both Tooker and Lopez and injured Silk, a Michigan citizen. Tooker's administrator (P) filed a wrongful death/personal injury action against Lopez' administrator (D) in New York state court. Lopez' administrator (D) raised as an affirmative defense Michigan's guest statute. Tooker's administrator (P) moved to strike the defense, contending that New York law applied as to that issue. The trial court granted the motion, and the appellate division affirmed. The N.Y. Court of Appeals granted review.

ISSUE: In a personal injury action in which all the parties are forum state citizens, will the guest statute of the jurisdiction of accident be applied?

HOLDING AND DECISION: (Keating, J.) No. In a personal injury action in which all the parties are forum state citizens, the guest statue of the jurisdiction of accident will not be applied. A provision of the law of the location of accident will not be applied if the forum state has a greater interest in the subject matter of the suit, and application of the law of the state of accident offends the forum state's public policy. Here, the accident, while occurring in Michigan, involved two New York citizens. [Silk, the Michigan citizen, was not a party to the present action.] The vehicle was registered and insured in New York. This shows that New York has a major interest in the outcome of this suit. With respect to policy, it is the stated policy of New York that all drivers be able to compensate victims of their torts. Enforcing a guest statue would contravene this policy, so such enforcement will not be allowed. Affirmed.

EDITOR'S ANALYSIS: Silk had not been a party to this suit but could have joined as a plaintiff. Had she done so, she would have been a "guest" for purposes of the Michigan guest statute. Michigan would have had a greater interest in her than the other parties. Under the courts' reasoning, the anomalous result would be possible that the statue could apply to one plaintiff, denying her a remedy, but not the other, who would be permitted to sue in New York.

[For more information on guest statutes, see Casenote Law Outline on Conflict of Laws, Chapter 6, § II, Modern Approaches.]

NOTES:

NEUMEIER v. KUEHNER

N.Y. Ct. App., 31 N.Y.2d 121, 325 N.Y.2d 64, 286 N.E.2d 454 (1972).

NATURE OF CASE: Appeal from dismissal of an affirmative defense in an action for wrongful death.

FACT SUMMARY: Kuehner's (D) decedent, a New York resident, drove into Canada to pick up Neumeier's (P) decedent, an Ontario resident, for an auto trip which was to be completed entirely within Ontario, but their car was struck by a Canadian National Railway (D) train, thus raising the question of whether Kuehner (D) could plead the Ontario guest statute as an affirmative defense.

CONCISE RULE OF LAW: For the forum state to apply its own law rather than that of the place of injury, the plaintiff must show that the forum state's connection with the action is sufficient to justify displacing the law of the place of injury.

FACTS: Kuehner's (D) decedent, a New York resident, drove into Canada to pick up Neumeier's (P) decedent, an Ontario resident, for an Ontario car trip that was to be completed entirely within the province of Ontario before Kuehner's (P) decedent returned home to New York. During the Ontario drive, the auto was struck by a train operated by the Canadian National Railway (D). Neumeier (P) brought suit in New York against Kuehner (D) and Railway (D). Both defendants pleaded the Ontario guest statute as a defense. The lower court dismissed the affirmative defense which led to this appeal.

ISSUE: For the forum state to apply its own law rather than that of the place of injury, must the plaintiff show that the forum state's connection with the action is sufficient to justify displacing the law of the place of injury?

HOLDING AND DECISION: (Fuld, C.J.) Yes. For the forum state to apply its own law rather than that of the place of injury, the plaintiff must show that the forum state's connection with the action is sufficient to justify displacing the law of the place of injury. Research has revealed "the distinct possibility that ... perhaps the only purpose of the (Ontario guest) statute was to protect owners and drivers against ungrateful guests." While New York has a strong interest in protecting its residents injured in a foreign state against unfair statutes of that state, it has no legitimate interest in ignoring that state's public policy and in protecting the plaintiff-guest domiciled and injured there from legislation directed to a resident riding in a vehicle traveling within its borders. While, in applying Ontario's guest statute to an Ontario-domiciled passenger, it is true that New York would be extending a "less generous right" to a New York insured resident, that is not invidious discrimination. Rather, it is the result of different rules held by different jurisdictions connected with the action. Thus, a general principle can be stated as follows: " . . . when the passenger and the driver are domiciled in different states, the applicable rule of decision will be that of the state of the accident

but not if it can be shown that displacing the normally applicable rule will advance the relevant substantive law purposes without impairing the smooth working of the multi-state system or producing great uncertainty for litigants." Thus, Ontario law should apply unless application of New York law would advance substantive law purposes, but New York's substantive law purposes would not be advanced because it would expose New York residents to greater liability than that imposed upon resident users of Ontario's highways. Conversely, failure to apply Ontario law would impair the smooth working of the multi-state system. Further, it would lead to uncertainty by encouraging forum shopping. As Ontario law must apply, the motion to dismiss the affirmative defense should have been denied. Reversed.

DISSENT: (Bergan, J.) "Neither because of `interest' nor `contact' nor any other defensible ground is it proper to say in a court of law that the rights of one man whose suit is accepted shall be adjudged differently on the merits on the basis of where he happens to live..."

EDITOR'S ANALYSIS: The rule C. J. Fuld sets forth was actually the third of three rules he suggests for handling guest statute conflicts problems. The first rule deals with the situation of driver and guest being domiciled in the same state and the car being registered there. In that case, the law of that state will determine the issues. The second rule involves a driver committing a tort in the state of his domicile for which that state does not impose liability. He should not be held liable because the law of the victim's state would impose on him liability. Conversely, when the guest's injury occurs in the state of his own domicile whose law permits recovery, the foreign driver should not be able to shield himself from liability by asserting his own state's law as a defense. The student should note that interest analysis rules have had heavy criticism raising the question of whether there should be rules or an approach.

[For more information on New York's "principles of preference" and Neumeier, see Casenote Law Outline on Conflict of Laws, Chapter 6, § II, Some Modern Approaches.]

NOTES:

SCHULTZ v. BOY SCOUTS OF AMERICA, INC.

N.Y. Ct. App., 65 N.Y.2d 189, 480 N.E.2d 679, (1985).

NATURE OF CASE: Review of dismissal of personal injury and wrongful death actions.

FACT SUMMARY: A personal injury/wrongful death action arose between New Jersey domiciliaries for acts occurring in New York and New Jersey.

CONCISE RULE OF LAW: The law of the place of injury will not be applied in a suit between co-domiciliaries of another jurisdiction, absent special circumstances.

FACTS: Richard (P) and Christopher Schultz were boys living in New Jersey. They attended a Franciscan-run school in that state. In July 1978, they attended, through a local Boy Scout (D) troop, a camp in New York. Brother Coakeley, a teacher at the school and also a scoutmaster, allegedly molested them at the camp and continued to do so after they returned to school. Christopher later committed suicide, and the investigation thereof brought out Brother Coakeley's acts. Christopher's parents (P) filed a wrongful death/personal injury action in New York against Boy Scouts of America, Inc. (D) and Brothers of the Poor of St. Francis, Inc. (D) for negligently hiring Brother Coakeley. Boy Scouts (D) was a New Jersey domiciliary; Brothers of the Poor (D) was organized in Ohio. The trial court, applying New Jersey law, invoked New Jersey's doctrine of charitable immunity and dismissed. The appellate division affirmed, and the N.Y. Court of Appeals granted review.

ISSUE: Absent special circumstances, will the law of the place of injury be applied in a suit between co-domiciliaries of another jurisdiction?

HOLDING AND DECISION: (Simons, J.) No. Absent special circumstances, the law of the place of injury will not be applied in a suit between co-domiciliaries of another jurisdiction. The traditional rule of choice of law was that the law of the place of injury would mechanistically be applied in a suit in a different forum. However, this method has been replaced with what has been called the "grouping of contacts" analysis, which seeks to compare the relative contacts that the involved jurisdiction have with the litigation. That jurisdiction with the greatest interests will have its law applied. The important consideration in this analysis is that not all contacts are of equal importance, and their respective importance depends on the nature of the case. When standard of conduct is at issue, the law of the place of the conduct is highly relevant. In matters involving allocation of loss, domicile is far more important. If a party chooses to reside in a jurisdiction, he accepts that the jurisdiction's rules regarding such allocation must be given great weight. When both plaintiff and defendant reside in the same jurisdiction, it would take an exceptional set of circumstances for that jurisdiction's rules regarding allocation of loss not to be applied. Here, all plaintiffs are New Jersey residents, as is the Boy Scouts (D). New Jersey has elected to favor charities by giving them immunity for simple negligence, and the litigants must accept their state's policy in this matter. As to the Franciscans (D), an Ohio organization, New Jersey appears to have a stronger interest in this matter than New York, so the result is the same. Affirmed.

DISSENT: (Jasen, J.) Boy Scouts of America (D) has since changed its residence to Texas, thus removing New Jersey's interest in protecting charities from relevant analysis.

EDITOR'S ANALYSIS: The position of the dissent is contrary to the weight of authority. Generally speaking, for conflict-of-law decisions, the domicile of the parties at the time of the injury is controlling. Post-injury changes of residence are not usually considered to be relevant.

[For more information on conflicts and torts, see Casenote Law Outline on Conflict of Laws, Chapter 6, § II, Modern Approaches.]

NOTES:

PADULA v. LILARN PROPERTIES CORPORATION
644 N.E.2d 1001, 620 N.Y.S.2d 310 (N.Y. Ct. App. 1994).

NATURE OF CASE: Review of allowed motion for partial summary judgment.

FACT SUMMARY: Padula (P) was injured while performing work on a construction project for Lilarn (D).

CONCISE RULE OF LAW: When parties share a common domicile, a determination as to whether the laws underlying the cause of action are primarily conduct regulating or loss allocating will determine which state law applies.

FACTS: Padula (P) is a resident of New York. Lilarn (D) is a corporation incorporated under the laws of New York. Padula (P) was injured when he fell from a scaffold while working on property owned by Lilarn (D) in Massachusetts. Padula (P) brought an action for damages alleging violations of the New York State Labor Law. Lilarn's (D) motion for partial summary judgment dismissing Padula's (P) action was granted by the Supreme Court of New York and affirmed by the Appellate Division. The New York Court of Appeals granted leave from the Supreme Court to bring up for review the Appellate Division's decision.

ISSUE: Are the labor laws at issue primarily conduct regulating or loss allocating?

HOLDING AND DECISION: (Smith, J.) The New York State Labor Law at issue is primarily conduct regulating, and therefore Massachusetts, and not New York, law should apply. New York choice of law principles begin the analysis. New York uses interest analysis to decide which jurisdiction has the greatest interest in having its law applied. To determine greater interest, the contacts in the jurisdiction are looked at, as well as whether the purpose of the law is to regulate conduct or allocate loss. That both parties were domiciled in New York and that the tort occurred in Massachusetts were considered. In regards to regulating conduct, the place of the tort governs, because that jurisdiction has the greatest interest in regulating behavior within its borders. In regards to those loss allocating rules which prohibit, assign, or limit liability after the tort occurs, the loss allocation rule of the common domicile applies. Since the New York State Labor Law at issue in this case was considered primarily to be conduct regulating, requiring that adequate safety measures be instituted at the worksite, Massachusetts law was properly applied. Affirmed.

EDITOR'S ANALYSIS: The state where the injury occurred in this case was determined by the court to have greater interests in having its law apply than the state where both parties shared a common domicile.

LILIENTHAL v. KAUFMAN
Or. Sup. Ct., 239 Or. 1, 395, P.2d 543 (1964).

NATURE OF CASE: Action to enforce payment of promissory notes.

FACT SUMMARY: Kaufman (D), an Oregon resident, had been declared a spendthrift under Oregon law and a guardian was appointed for his protection. He went to California, where he borrowed money from Lilienthal (P) to finance a business venture. Kaufman's (D) guardian now defends an action to collect the loans on the basis that the contracts were invalid because of the guardianship.

CONCISE RULE OF LAW: Where two states have an equal balance of interests in application of their own laws to an interstate contract dispute, the forum is privileged to apply its own law so as to advance its own public policy.

FACTS: Under a statutory procedure in Oregon, Kaufman (D) had been declared a spendthrift and a guardian appointed to manage his affairs to prevent waste of his assets to the detriment of himself and his family. By the terms of the statute, any contracts made by the spendthrift after the appointment of the guardian were voidable by the guardian. Kaufman (D) traveled from his home in Oregon to San Francisco where he induced Lilienthal (P) to advance him money for a business venture. Lilienthal (P) was unaware of Kaufman's (D) disability and when he sought to enforce repayment of the promissory notes in an Oregon court, the guardian declared the obligations void and unenforceable. California law did not recognize a spendthrift's liability to contract.

ISSUE: May the forum apply its own law to advance its own public policy where there is an equal balance of conflicting interests in the choice of law in an interstate contract dispute?

HOLDING AND DECISION: (Denecke, J.) Yes. In a previous case involving Kaufman (D) as a defendant in a similar suit brought by an Oregon resident, this court held that the guardianship acted as a bar to enforcement of the obligations. The court is now faced, however, with the conflicting interests of California in protecting its own creditors. Further, there is the traditional rule that the law of the place where a contract is made will govern its validity. There is authority for the assertion that choice of law should be made in a manner that upholds, not voids, a contract. Oregon has an interest in seeing that contracts made by its citizens are honored in Oregon courts. Balanced against these considerations is the valid public policy, expressed by the legislation, of preventing a spendthrift from making himself and his family public charges by his wastrel ways. The Oregon legislation must be presumed to have considered the adverse consequences of the spendthrift disability on interstate commerce when choosing to grant this form of immunity. When faced with such an equal balance of interests, the courts of this state are under an obligation to give force to the express public policy. Toward that end we find the obligations unenforceable.

EDITOR'S ANALYSIS: The case represents an example of Currie's approach to choice of law that emphasizes the importance of the forum's law. The Oregon court was quick to find that there was a balance of conflicting interests, and that the forum should prevail. There has been criticism of this case on the ground that, while an Oregon creditor is presumed to know Oregon law, a California creditor must be presumed to act on his knowledge of California law. The Oregon statute is not so commonplace as to be regarded as within the reasonable contemplation of the out-of-state creditor.

[For more information on governmental interest analysis in contracts cases, see Casenote Law Outline on Conflict of Laws, Chapter 7, Contracts, § II, Some Modern Approaches.]

NOTES:

BERNKRANT v. FOWLER
55 Cal. 2d 588, 360 P.2d 906 (1961).

NATURE OF CASE: Review of order dismissing action to cancel a note.

FACT SUMMARY: Fowler (D) contended that California's Statute of Frauds should be applied to an extraterritorial oral agreement.

CONCISE RULE OF LAW: A local Statute of Frauds will not be applied to an extraterritorial oral agreement.

FACTS: The Berkrants (P) purchased certain real estate from Fowler's (D) predessor, Granrud. Subsequent to this, the Berkrants (P) and Granrud agreed that, in exchange for certain acts by the Berkrants (P), Granrud would by will forgive any remaining debt concerning the property. The property was situated in Nevada. The Berkrants (P) were Nevada citizens. Granrud's citizenship was unclear. After Granrud's death his will contained no debt forgiveness. The Berkrants (P) brought an action in California State Court seeking to have the note canceled. Fowler (D) contended that California's Statute of Frauds made the oral agreement unenforceable. The Berkrants (P) contended that Nevada's statute, which would not void the agreement, was the applicable law. The trial court applied the California statue and dismissed. The California Supreme Court granted review.

ISSUE: Will a local Statute of Frauds be applied to an extraterritorial oral agreement?

HOLDING AND DECISION: (Traynor, J.) No. A local Statute of Frauds will not be applied to an extraterritorial oral agreement. Parties to a local agreement cannot reasonably be expected to take cognizance of the law of all the other jurisdictions where either the subject matter of the agreement or the parties thereto might later go. When multiple jurisdictions are implicated in an action, a court must decide which jurisdiction has the stronger interest. When the transaction is purely local, that locality's law must be applied. Here, the property was located in Nevada, and the Berkrants (P) were Nevada citizens. Although Granrud moved to California later in life, his citizenship at the time of the agreement was unknown. Therefore, only Nevada had an interest in the oral agreement, and its law should have been applied. Reversed.

EDITOR'S ANALYSIS: There is such a thing as a false conflict of laws, and the present opinion is an example thereof. In a true conflict case, two or more states have a legitimate interest in having their own law applied. In a false conflict case, only one state has such an interest, even though the case, through some fortuity, is being litigated in another state.

[For more information on false conflicts, see Casenote Law Outline on Conflict of Laws, Chapter 5, § III, Characterizing the Issues.]

NOTES:

HURTADO v. SUPERIOR COURT
Cal. Sup. Ct., 11 Cal. 3d 574, 522 P.2d 666 (1974).

NATURE OF CASE: Review of order denying petition for mandamus in a wrongful death action.

FACT SUMMARY: Hurtado (D), a California resident, contended that California should not apply its law allowing unlimited recovery for wrongful death because the plaintiffs were not California residents.

CONCISE RULE OF LAW: California may apply its law permitting unlimited recovery for wrongful death, even if the plaintiffs are not California residents.

FACTS: Hurtado (D), a California resident, was involved in an accident in California which resulted in the death of a resident of Mexico. The decedent's survivors were also Mexican residents. Mexico had a statutory cap on damages for wrongful death; California allowed unlimited recovery. In the survivors' wrongful death action, the trial court held that California's law applied. Hurtado (D) petitioned the state court of appeal for a writ of mandamus compelling the trial court to apply Mexican law. The writ was denied, and the California Supreme Court granted review.

ISSUE: May California apply its law permitting unlimited recovery for wrongful death even if the plaintiffs are not California residents?

HOLDING AND DECISION: (Sullivan, J.) Yes. California may apply its law permitting unlimited recovery for wrongful death, even if the plaintiffs are not California residents. California, as the forum state, should apply its own law unless another state has a greater governmental interest in having its law applied. Mexico's cap on wrongful death awards reflects a desire to protect Mexican defendants from perceived excessive liability for wrongful death. When the defendants in an action are not Mexican, Mexico has no interest in having its law applied. This alone is sufficient to justify use of California law. However, California has an articulable interest in having its law applied. A major purpose of unlimited liability is to deter the kind of conduct resulting in death. Whether plaintiffs are Californian or not bears no relation to this interest. For these reasons, California law was properly applied here. Affirmed.

EDITOR'S ANALYSIS: Sometimes courts will go through a rather thorough legal analysis to achieve a result when, in fact, it is merely trying to prevent a perceived injustice. It is possible that this was occurring here. Had Mexican law been applied, the damage cap would have been less than $2,000. This is a minuscule recovery for wrongful death by California standards, and no doubt the court was not inclined to seeing it imposed.

[For more information on governmental interest analysis, see Casenote Law Outline on Conflict of Laws, Chapter 6, § II, Modern Approaches.]
NOTES:

BERNHARD v. HARRAH'S CLUB
16 Cal.3d 313, P.2d 719 (1976).

NATURE OF CASE: Action for damages for injuries sustained.

FACT SUMMARY: Bernhard (P) attempted to hold Harrah's (D), a Nevada corporation, responsible for the injuries he sustained in a California accident with a California driver who had become intoxicated while being served drinks at Harrah's (D) establishment in Nevada.

CONCISE RULE OF LAW: True conflicts should be resolved by applying the law of the state whose interest would be the more impaired if its law were not applied.

FACTS: Harrah's (D), a Nevada corporation, solicited business for its Nevada establishment by advertising in California. In response to such, the Myers, California residents, drove to Harrah's (D) and became intoxicated from the drinks they were served. While still intoxicated, they headed home. On a California freeway, their car drifted across the center line and collided head-on with a motorcycle being driven by Bernhard (D), a California resident. He brought suit in California to recover for the injuries he sustained, contending that California law gave him an action against Harrah's (D) and should be applied. Harrah's (D) argued that Nevada law applied, which denies recovery against a tavern keeper by a third person for injuries proximately caused by the former selling or furnishing alcoholic beverages to an intoxicated person who inflicts injuries on the latter. Bernhard (P) appealed when the court sustained the demurrer Harrah's (D) filed.

ISSUE: In the case of a true conflict, should the court apply the law of the state whose interest would be the more impaired if the law were not applied?

HOLDING AND DECISION: (Sullivan, J.) Yes. In those cases where a true conflict is shown to exist, this court's approach is to apply the law of the state whose interest would be the more impaired if its law were not applied. No longer do the courts adhere to the once-traditional rule that the law of the place of the wrong should automatically govern. Nevada's interest is in protecting its tavern keepers from civil liability. However, Harrah's (D) solicited California business and thus put itself at the heart of California's regulatory interest, namely to prevent tavern keepers from selling alcoholic beverages to obviously intoxicated persons who are likely to act in California in the intoxicated state. Between Nevada and California, California is that state whose interest would be more impaired if its law were not applied. Thus, California law must govern. Reversed and remanded.

EDITOR'S ANALYSIS: So far, only California has adopted this "comparative impairment" approach. It was designed to avoid the problems inherent in attempting to resolve a conflict by deciding which state's law reflects the better or worthier policy, as other approaches do.

[For more information on comparative conflicts tests in torts cases, see Casenote Law Outline on Conflict of Laws, Chapter 6, Torts, § II, Modern Approaches.]

NOTES:

MILKOVICH v. SAARI
295 Minn. 155, 203 N.W.2d 408 (1973).

NATURE OF CASE: Appeal of order denying motion to dismiss and striking affirmative defense in action for damages for personal injury.

FACT SUMMARY: Saari (D), sued in Minnesota by her auto passenger Milkovich (P), contended that Minnesota should apply Ontario's guest statue.

CONCISE RULE OF LAW: Minnesota will not apply a foreign guest statute.

FACTS: Milkovich (P) and Saari (D) were both citizens of Ontario, Canada. While driving in Minnesota, Saari (D) lost control of her vehicle, which then slid off the road. Milkovich (P), who suffered serious injuries requiring hospitalization for one and a half months, sued Saari (D) in Minnesota state court. Saari (D) moved to dismiss, based on Ontario's guest statute, which required a showing of gross negligence on the part of a driver. The motion was denied, and Saari's (D) affirmative defense based on the statute was stricken. Saari (D) appealed.

ISSUE: Will Minnesota apply a foreign guest statute?

HOLDING AND DECISION: (Todd, J.) No. Minnesota will not apply a foreign guest statute. In early days, the law of the place of injury used to be controlling. However, this "lex loci" approach has been replaced with an analysis involving five factors: (1) predictability of results, (2) maintenance of interstate and international order, (3) simplification of the judiciary's tastes, (4) advancement of the forum's governmental interests, and (5) application of the better rule of law. In a tort action, the first three factors are of lesser importance than the latter two. In fact, these two tend to meld together, as the forum has an interest in applying the better rule of law. This court believes that guest statutes, which are based on vague concerns about collusive lawsuits and the impropriety of a guest suing a host, are bad law, unworthy of adoption in this state. For this reason under the analysis outlined above, it will not be applied in Minnesota. Affirmed.

DISSENT: (Peterson, J.) The appropriate test is the "center-of-gravity" test. Here, all interests center on Ontario, as the litigants live there and the auto is registered and garaged there.

EDITOR'S ANALYSIS: The first factor cited by the court, predictability, relates more to contract law than tort law. Torts, by their nature, are unpredictable. Predictability is a more realistic goal in the contractual arena, where parties have more freedom in structuring their situation.

[For more information on tort choice of law, see Casenote Law Outline on Conflict of Laws, Chapter 6, § II, Modern Approaches.]

NOTES:

PHILLIPS v. GENERAL MOTORS CORP.
Decedents' estate (P) v. Manufacturer (D)
Mont. Sup. Ct., 298 Mont. 438, 995 P.2d 1002 (2000).

NATURE OF CASE: Certified questions regarding Montana's choice of law rule.

FACT SUMMARY: Phillips (P), the legal guardian of the sole survivor of a traffic accident and personal representative of the estates of the survivor's parents who perished in the crash, sued General Motors (GM) (D) for personal injury, product liability, and wrongful death in Montana, where the accident victims resided.

CONCISE RULE OF LAW: Where there is a potential conflict of laws, Montana will follow the most significant relationship test in determining which state's substantive law to apply.

FACTS: Phillips (P) represented the estates of a Montana family killed while driving a Chevrolet pickup truck on a freeway in Kansas while on the way to spend Christmas in North Carolina. Phillips (P), who lived in North Carolina, filed suit for product liability in federal court in Montana. When the parties disagreed on which state's substantive law applied, the court certified three questions to the Montana Supreme Court.

ISSUE: Where there is a potential conflict of laws, will Montana follow the most significant relationship test in determining which state's substantive law to apply?

HOLDING AND DECISION: (Regnier, J.) Yes. Where there is a potential conflict of laws, Montana will follow the most significant relationship test in determining which state's substantive law to apply. Under the Restatement (Second) of Conflict of Laws approach that the Court now adopts, the local law of the place of injury, Kansas, is presumptively applicable in a product liability and wrongful death action unless another state has a more significant relationship. The following factors all point to the application of Montana law: the deceased resided in Montana at the time of the accident; GM (D) does business in Montana; and Montana has a direct interest in preventing defective products from injuring Montana residents and is interested in fully compensating Montana residents. The public policies of all interested states must be considered in determining which state has the more significant relationship; a "public policy" exception would therefore be redundant. Since the lex loci rule has been abandoned for contract disputes, the same choice of law approach should also be applied in tort cases.

EDITOR'S ANALYSIS: The court carefully considered each of the factors set out in Restatement (Second). They included: needs of the interstate and international system, the policies of interested states, place of injury, place of conduct, residence of parties, and basic policies underlying the particular field of law.

North Carolina would not have applied its own laws because it still adhered to the traditional place of injury rule in tort cases.

QUICKNOTES
PRODUCT LIABILITY - The legal liability of manufacturers and sellers for damages and injuries suffered by buyers, users, and even bystanders because of defects in goods purchased.

LEX LOCI - The law of the place governs the substantive rights of parties to an action.

NEDLLOYD LINES B.V. v. SUPERIOR COURT OF SAN MATEO COUNTY SEAWINDS LTD.

Ca. Sup. Ct., 3 Cal. 4th 459, 834 P.2d 1148 (1992).

NATURE OF CASE: Review of denial of a demurrer to a complaint alleging breach of contract, breach of the implied covenant of good faith and fair dealing, and breach of fiduciary duty.

FACT SUMMARY: When Nedlloyd (D) demurred to a complaint brought by Seawinds (P) and argued that the contract between the two parties required the application of Hong Kong law to Seawinds' (P) claims, Seawinds (P) responded that California law should be applied.

CONCISE RULE OF LAW: A contractual choice-of-law provision is enforceable and encompasses all causes of action arising from or related to the agreement.

FACTS: Nedlloyd Lines (D), a shipping company incorporated in the Netherlands with its principal place of business in Rotterdam, and other partners, including a Hong Kong corporation, entered into a contract to purchase shares of stock in Seawinds (P), a shipping company that operated three container ships. Seawinds (P) was incorporated in Hong Kong and had its principal place of business in Redwood City, California. The contract, to finance and operate an international shipping business, contained a choice-of-law clause stating that the agreement was to be governed by and construed in accordance with Hong Kong law. Six years later, Seawinds (P) sued Nedlloyd (D) for (1) breach of contract, (2) breach of the implied covenant of good faith and fair dealing, and (3) breach of fiduciary duty. Nedlloyd (D) demurred to Seawinds' (P) complaint on the grounds that it failed to state causes of action for counts (2) and (3) and also argued that the contract required the application of Hong Kong law to Seawinds' (P) claims. Seawinds (P) argued that California law should be applied to its causes of action, and both the trial court and the court of appeal ruled in favor of Seawinds (P). The California Supreme Court granted review.

ISSUE: Is a contractual choice-of-law provision enforceable and does it encompass all causes of action arising from or related to the agreement?

HOLDING AND DECISION: (Baxter, J.) Yes. A contractual choice-of-law provision is enforceable and encompasses all causes of action arising from or related to the agreement. In determining the enforceability of arm's-length contractual choice-of-law provisions, California courts shall apply the principles set forth in Restatement (Second) of Conflicts, § 187, which reflects a strong policy favoring enforcement of such provisions. Section 187 provides that the law of the state chosen by the parties applies unless it has no substantial relationship to the parties or the transaction and there is no other reasonable basis for the parties' choice. Here, Hong Kong, the chosen state, clearly has a "substantial relationship to the parties," as Seawinds (P) is incorporated there

and has a registered office there, as does one of the shareholder parties to the agreement. Moreover, the presence of two Hong Kong corporations as parties also provides a "reasonable basis" for such a contractual provision. Second, Seawinds (P) has not identified any fundamental policy requiring the application of California law to its causes of action. Furthermore, a valid choice-of-law clause, which provides that a specified body of law "governs" the "agreement" between the parties, encompasses all causes of action arising from or related to the agreement. Common sense and commercial reality necessitate that when two sophisticated, commercial entities agree to a choice-of-law clause like this one, the most reasonable interpretation of their actions is that they intended for the clause to apply to all such causes of action. Reversed and remanded.

CONCURRENCE: (Kennard, J.) California occupies a position of leadership in international trade, and it is in the interest of this state and its residents that transactions with international aspects not be discouraged. In this case, the "substantial relationship" requirement is satisfied, and California's interest in respecting the parties' choice-of-law agreement is at least as strong as its interest in applying its substantive law. Because California's interest in enforcing its substantive law is not materially greater than Hong Kong's, we need not reach the question of whether application of Hong Kong's law would be contrary to a fundamental policy of California.

DISSENT: (Panelli, J.) The majority's analysis of the scope of the choice-of-law clause to cover noncontractual causes of action, such as Seawinds' (P) breach of fiduciary duty claim, is unsound. It is based solely on common sense and commercial reality; no authority for the rule is cited. Further, the majority's rule chooses predictability over the intent of the parties in spite of a state statute which requires that a contract must be interpreted to give effect to the mutual intention of the parties as of the time of contracting.

EDITOR'S ANALYSIS: The majority had no patience for what it saw as Seawinds' (P) contrived postdispute litigation strategy of attempting to apply California law to determine predispute contractual intent on the choice-of-law clause. The primary purpose of a choice-of-law provision was to avoid "uncertainty and ambiguity," according to the majority, and they were not going to permit Seawinds (P) to muddy the waters with extensive litigation of the parties' supposed intentions regarding the clause.

[For more information on choice of law, see Casenote Law Outline on Conflict of Laws, Chapter 1, § III, Choice of Law.]

NOTES:

BANEK, INC. v. YOGURT VENTURES U.S.A., INC.
6 F.3d 357 (6th Cir. 1993).

NATURE OF CASE: Interlocutory appeal of ruling that a choice of law provision contained in a franchise agreement was valid and enforceable.

FACT SUMMARY: Banek (P) sued Yogurt (D) for breach contract, violations of various laws and rules, fraud, misrepresentation, and negligence. Yogurt's (D) motion for dismissal was granted.

CONCISE RULE OF LAW: A choice of law clause will be found valid unless the legislature prohibits it. The clause will be enforceable under Michigan's choice of law provisions if there is a substantial relationship between the parties and the choice of law clause state and if Michigan's public policy concerns are not offended. The clause at issue was sufficiently broad to encompass all of Plaintiff's claims.

FACTS: Banek (P) entered into negotiations with Yogurt (D), a Georgia corporation, for the purchase of a yogurt franchise to be located in Michigan. Prior to the parties' executing a Franchise and Development Agreement, several changes had been made to it. About two years later, Banek (P) closed its franchise and sued Yogurt (D) in Michigan state court for breach of contract, various violations of the Michigan Franchise Investment Law, violations of the Federal Trade Commission Franchise Rules, common law fraud and misrepresentation, and negligence. The case was moved to federal court based on diversity jurisdiction, and Yogurt (D) moved to dismiss. The district court granted the motion in part, ruling that the choice of law provision in the agreement providing that Georgia law was to govern was valid and enforceable under Michigan law. Appealed.

ISSUE: Is a choice of law clause valid and enforceable under Michigan choice of law rules such that Georgia law governs all claims?

HOLDING AND DECISION: (Guy, J.) Yes. The clause is valid and enforceable under Michigan choice-of-law rules, and Georgia law governs all claims. The choice of law clause does not operate as a waiver of the rights and protections under the Michigan Franchise Investment Law. The Michigan legislature was specific enough to include forum selection provisions in the list of void provisions but did not specify choice of law provisions. Michigan, therefore, did not express a desire to void choice of law provisions, perhaps because other states' laws may provide more protection to franchisees or because of cost to franchisors in conforming to different laws. In addition, the parties may contract for a particular state's law to apply. The contractual choice of law provision will govern in this case because there is a substantial relationship between the parties and Georgia and because Michigan public policy would not be offended on the basis of overreaching by Yogurt (D) and unequal bargaining power of the parties. This was not an adhesion contract, but rather there was negotiation as to its terms. In addition, it was not shown that there were significant differences in the application of the law to the claims of the two states. Plaintiff had various remedies under Georgia law. Application of one state's laws was not shown to violate a specific fundamental policy of another state. Georgia law governs all claims because the choice of law provision was sufficiently broad to cover all claims and the claims were not just tangentially related to the franchise relationship. Affirmed.

EDITOR'S ANALYSIS: In general, courts are hesitant to not enforce choice of law provisions in contracts freely bargained for by the parties, especially if the legislature does not prohibit such clauses.

KIPIN INDUSTRIES, INC. v.
VAN DEILEN INTERNATIONAL, INC.
182 F.3d 490 (6th Cir. 1999).

NATURE OF CASE: Appeal from motion to release bonds.

FACT SUMMARY: Kipin (P) was trying to recover bonds based on some liens that it previously had against Van Deilen's (D) interests. Van Deilen (D) moved to release the bonds based on a clause in a contract between the parties which prevented the filing of such liens.

CONCISE RULE OF LAW: A choice of law contractual provision will be honored by the court if there is a substantial relationship between the chosen state and the contract and if the application of the chosen state's law doesn't violate a fundamental policy of a state having a greater interest in the dispute, which state would have been the governing law absent the provision. If, however, under the Restatement, the parties' choice of law is to be considered a mistake because the chosen law would invalidate an express provision of the contract, then the chosen law would not apply.

FACTS: Kipin (P) and Van Deilen (D) entered into a contract under which Kipin (P) agreed to perform work in Kentucky at a site owned by A.K. Steel, Inc. Kipin (P) filed suit in federal court in Pennsylvania to recover money owed it. Per the contract's forum selection clause, the case was transferred to federal court in Michigan. Kipin (P) subsequently filed liens against A.K. Steel's property. A clause in the contract, however, prevented the filing of such liens. Van Deilen (D) filed bonds in Kentucky that discharged Kipin's (P) liens. Kipin (P) filed this action to recover on the bonds. Pointing to the lien-waiver provision of the contract, Van Deilen (D) moved to release the bonds. The district court held that the lien-waiver provision was enforceable and granted Van Deilen's (D) motion. Kipin (P) appealed.

ISSUE: Is a lien-waiver provision in a contract enforceable when the contract contains a choice of law provision which, when applied, would void the lien waiver provision?

HOLDING AND DECISION: (Moore, J.) Yes. Although the express waiver provision would be void under the substantive law of the chosen choice of law state, Michigan, the waiver is valid under the law of Kentucky which would govern the agreement in the absence of an express choice of law provision. With respect to the lien-waiver issue, Kentucky has the most significant relationship to the transaction and parties. The substantive law of Michigan applies generally to the contract, but it doesn't invalidate the express waiver in this circumstance. In addition to ignoring the mistaken choice of law provision and enforcing the express contractual provision, the relationship between the chosen state and the contract, as well as whether a policy of the non-choice state would be violated, must be considered to determine the enforceability of a contractual provision. In this case the place of domicile is sufficient to meet the substantial relationship test. Furthermore, it is not considered a fundamental policy of Kentucky to permit parties to waive the rights to place liens. The Restatement indicated that when the express provisions would be valid under the law of the state that would govern in the absence of a conflict of law provision, the selection of an incompatible state law to govern the contract is to be disregarded as a mistake by the parties. Affirmed.

EDITOR'S ANALYSIS: Generally, choice of law provisions will be honored unless there is no relationship between the state and the contract, a fundamental policy of the non-choice state would be violated, or there is a mistaken choice of law provision.

REICH v. PURCELL
67 Cal. 2d 551, 442 P.2d 727 (1967).

NATURE OF CASE: Appeal from award of damages for wrongful death.

FACT SUMMARY: The Reichs (P) moved to California after the incident giving rise to a suit they later filed there.

CONCISE RULE OF LAW: The relocation of a party to a state after the event giving rise to a suit is not a factor to be considered in deciding which law to apply.

FACTS: Ms. Reich and her two sons were in a fatal automobile accident with Purcell (D) while driving in Missouri. They were Ohio residents; Purcell (D) was a California resident. Ms. Reich and one son were killed, and the other son was injured. Mr. Reich (P) brought a wrongful death suit; Jeffrey Reich (P), the surviving son, filed a wrongful death and personal injury suit. The suit was filed in California, where they had moved after the accident. Purcell (D) argued that Missouri law should apply. Missouri had a $25,000 cap on wrongful death awards. The trial court held Missouri law to apply and entered a wrongful death award of $25,000. The Reichs (P) appealed, contending that California or Ohio law should apply.

ISSUE: Is the relocation of a party to a state after the event giving rise to a suit a factor to be considered in deciding which law to apply?

HOLDING AND DECISION: (Traynor, C.J.) No. The relocation of a party to a state after the event giving rise to a suit is not a factor to be considered in deciding which law to apply. Changes of residence occurring after a cause of action arises cannot be considered relevant in deciding which jurisdictions law to apply. First, to hold otherwise would be to permit forum-shopping. Second, an after-the-fact migration to a state does not increase that state's governmental interest in having its law applied. Consequently, the Reichs' (P) postaccident relocation to California does not create a reason to apply California law. [The court went on, for reasons not cited in the casebook excerpt, to hold Ohio's law to be applicable rather than Missouri's.]

EDITOR'S ANALYSIS: After-acquired domicile can sometimes present itself in ways not as easy to resolve as it was in the present case. One example occurs in tort law when a party had formulated an intent to relocate prior to an accident but does not relocate until afterward. Another example, this occurring in contract law, is a relocation occurring between contract formation and a cause of action occurring thereon.

[For more information on choice and domicile, see Casenote Law Outline on Conflict of Laws, Chapter 6, § II, Modern Approaches.]

NOTES:

PFAU v. TRENT ALUMINUM CO.
55 N.J. 511, 263 A.2d 129 (1970).

NATURE OF CASE: Review of order reversing order striking an affirmative defense in a personal injury action.

FACT SUMMARY: Trent Aluminum (D), sued for personal injury, contended that a foreign state's choice-of-law rule should be applied if its substantive law were to be applied.

CONCISE RULE OF LAW: A state's substantive law may be applied without its choice-of-law rules also being applied.

FACTS: Pfau (P) and Trent (D) were schoolmates at college in Iowa. Trent (D) was a New Jersey citizen and Pfau (P) a Connecticut citizen. While driving a vehicle belonging to his father's company, Trent Aluminum Co. (D), Trent (D) was involved in an auto accident in Iowa. Pfau (P) was a passenger in the vehicle. Trent Aluminum (D) contended that Iowa's guest statute applied, and raised this defense. Pfau (P) successfully moved to strike the defense, the court ruling Connecticut law, which contained no guest statute to be applicable. The court of appeals reversed, holding Connecticut's choice-of-law rule also to apply. Since Connecticut applied the lex loci rule, the court held Iowa law applicable. The New Jersey Supreme Court granted review.

ISSUE: May a state's substantive law be applied without its choice-of-law rules also being applied?

HOLDING AND DECISION: (Proctor, J.) Yes. A state's substantive law may be applied without its choice-of-law rules also being applied. Choice-of-law analysis is based on governmental interests, and a nonforum state's choice-of-law rule does not relate to its substantive interests in a litigation. This is particularly true when a state adheres to the lex loci rule, which has nothing at all to do with governmental interests. Consequently, applying Connecticut's choice-of-law rule would not promote any of its governmental interests in this litigation and should not be applied. [The court went on to hold that since connecticut and New Jersey had identical law on the guest statute issue, there was no conflict to resolve.] Reversed.

EDITOR'S ANALYSIS: Some commentators have not taken the position apparently held here that choice-of-law rules are not relevant in a governmental interest analysis. Some have held, for instance, that choice-of-law rules can illustrate what precisely a states' governmental interests might be, as such interests are likely to be incorporated into choice-of-law rules. This debate has largely been theoretical; as a practical matter, a forum state's choice-of-law rules are almost always used.

[For more information on substantive law, see **Casenote Law Outline on Conflict of Laws, Chapter 5, § II, Classifying Rules as Substantive or Procedural.]**

NOTES:

RICHARDS v. UNITED STATES
369 U.S. 1 (1962).

NATURE OF CASE: Review of dismissal of wrongful death action.

FACT SUMMARY: In an action brought under the FTCA, Richards (P) argued that only the internal law of the place of negligence should be applied.

CONCISE RULE OF LAW: In choosing applicable law under the FTCA, the whole law of the place of negligence controls.

FACTS: An airplane crash occurred in Missouri, resulting in numerous deaths. A suit was brought against the Government (D) on the theory of improper regulation by the FAA. It was disputed that the acts allegedly constituting negligence had occurred in Oklahoma. In construing the Federal Tort Claims Act (FTCA), the district court held that the whole law of Oklahoma applied, and under Oklahoma's choice-of-law rules, Missouri law applied. Since Missouri provided for a cap on wrongful death awards, and the various plaintiffs had already recovered more than that amount, the court dismissed Richards' (P) action. The court of appeals affirmed, and the Supreme Court granted review.

ISSUE: In choosing applicable law under the FTCA, does the whole law of the place of negligence control?

HOLDING AND DECISION: (Warren, C.J.) Yes. In choosing applicable law under the FTCA, the whole law of the place of negligence controls. The FTCA makes applicable the "law of the place where the act or omission occurred." The statute does not specify whether the whole law of such place should be applied or only the internal law. However, when read in the context of the FTCA in its entirety, it appears clear that the whole law should be applied. It is the purpose of the FTCA to put the federal government in the same place as a private tort litigant, with several narrow exceptions. Since a private litigant would be subject to the whole law of a jurisdiction, so too should the Government (D). Further, by failing to adopt a federal conflict-of-law framework for federal tort claims, it appears that Congress preferred to leave the matter to the states. The whole-law approach better achieves this purpose. For these reasons, the district court properly applied the law of Missouri. Affirmed.

EDITOR'S ANALYSIS: Conflicts cases in federal court often involve two different levels. The first is whether federal or state law will be applied. The second is which state law to apply, if any. The present case was an exception, as no federal substantive law was involved.

[For more information on renvoi, see Casenote Law Outline on Conflict of Laws, Chapter 5, § IV, Dealing with Renvoi.]

NOTES:

LEDESMA v. JACK STEWART PRODUCE, INC.
816 F.2d 482 (9th Cir. 1987).

NATURE OF CASE: Appeal of order dismissing personal injury action.

FACT SUMMARY: The federal district court held that the statute of limitations of the forum state, California, had to be applied in a personal injury action arising from an Arizona car accident that involved Arkansas and California residents.

CONCISE RULE OF LAW: A forum state's statute of limitations will not necessarily be applied in a tort action.

FACTS: Several California residents were involved in a motor vehicle accident in Arizona with Mize (D), an Arkansas resident. The vehicle was owned by an Oklahoma corporation, Jack Stewart Produce, Inc. (D). The injured Californians, Ledesma (P), Rodriguez (P), Gaytan (P), and Santiago (P), filed a tort action in U.S. district court, jurisdiction based on diversity. The court, holding forum state law to be necessarily applicable, dismissed on statute of limitations grounds. Ledesma (P) appealed.

ISSUE: Will a forum state's statute of limitations necessarily be applied in a tort action?

HOLDING AND DECISION: (Nelson, J.) No. A forum state's statute of limitations will not necessarily be applied in a tort action. The law of the forum state regarding conflicts of law is to be utilized in any applicable situation. California has adopted the "governmental interest" test. This test involves an analysis of whether a conflict in fact exists and, if so, an analysis of which state's interest would be more impaired if its law were not given effect. Here, California's interest in its relatively short statute of limitations is to protect resident defendants. This is inapplicable here because Jack Stewart (D) is not a California resident. Arizona's interest in providing a cause of action is to prevent tortious conduct within the state. This policy will be impaired if a foreign, shorter statute is applied to a cause of action that arose there. Consequently, under the governmental interest analysis, the law of Arizona should be applied in this case. Reversed.

DISSENT: (Noonan, J.) The Restatement makes it clear that the statute of the forum will always be applied.

EDITOR'S ANALYSIS: This opinion appears to be at odds with the usual analysis for statutes of limitations in conflict cases. Statutes of limitations are usually classified as procedural rules, and forum state procedural rules are usually applicable. The Restatement, at § 142(i), reflects this view.

[For more information on statutes of limitations, see Casenote Law Outline on Conflict of Laws, Chapter 5, § II, Classifying Rules as Substantive or Procedural.]

NOTES:

GLOBAL FINANCIAL CORP. v. TRIARC CORP.
93 N.Y.2d 525, 715 N.E.2d 482 (1999).

NATURE OF CASE: Appeal from dismissal of contract and quantum meriut claims.

FACT SUMMARY: Global (P) sued Triarc (D) in New York to recover commissions and fees for consulting services it rendered.

CONCISE RULE OF LAW: The statute of limitations of a foreign jurisdiction is used to determine when a nonresident cause of action accrues, if that limitations period is shorter than the nonforeign jurisdiction. A cause of action will accrue for a party where it suffered injury, which is usually its place of residence.

FACTS: Triarc Corp. (D) retained Global (P) to perform consulting services. Global (P) brought suit in the Supreme Court, New York County, to recover its commission and fees. Triarc (D) moved to dismiss for failing to come within the statute of limitations of Delaware (where Plaintiff was incorporated) or Pennsylvania (where Plaintiff had its principal place of business). Plaintiff's claims would have been time-barred in both states. Global (P) argued that the New York statute of limitations should apply because most of the events relating to the contract took place in New York. The Supreme Court dismissed the complaint. The Appellate Division affirmed, and Plaintiff appealed.

ISSUE: Does a nonresident plaintiff's contract and quantum meruit claims accrue in New York, where most of the relevant events occurred, rather than in the plaintiff's state of residence where it sustained the economic impact of the breach?

HOLDING AND DECISION: (Kaye, J.) No. A plaintiff's contract and quantum meruit claims will accrue not where most of the relevant events occurred but where it sustains the economic impact of the breach. The Plaintiff's claims accrued in Pennsylvania or Delaware. The statute of limitations of a foreign jurisdiction is used when a non-resident cause of action accrued, if that limitations period is shorter than the nonforeign jurisdiction. In this case, therefore, Global's (P) claims accrued not where most of the relevant events occurred, but in Global's state of residence where it sustained the economic impact of the breach. Global (P) argued that New York law applied because its claims accrued in New York where the contract was negotiated, executed, mostly performed, and breached. There is a difference, however, between choice-of-law, which is a matter of common law, and the statute of limitations, which is a statute. Accrued means the time and the place where the plaintiff first had the right to bring the cause of action. "Center of gravity" and "interest analysis" choice-of-law analyses are inapplicable to the question of statutory construction. The traditional definition of accrual applies here, and a cause of action accrues at the time and in the place of the injury. An injury is usually where the plaintiff resides and sustains the economic impact of the loss. Affirmed.

EDITOR'S ANALYSIS: For statute of limitations purposes, the place of the injury is used, not traditional choice-of-law considerations.

PAUL v. NATIONAL LIFE

W. Va. Sup. Ct., 352 S.E.2d 550 (1986).

NATURE OF CASE: Appeal of dismissal of wrongful death action.

FACT SUMMARY: Paul (P) contended that the doctrine of lex loci delicti should be abandoned.

CONCISE RULE OF LAW: The doctrine of lex loci delicti should not be abandoned.

FACTS: Paul was a passenger in a vehicle driven by Vickers. Both were West Virginia residents. While in Indiana, Vickers lost control of the vehicle, and a collision ensued. Both were killed. Paul (P), as administrator of Paul's estate, brought a wrongful death action against Vickers' successor. The trial court, applying the law of Indiana, dismissed based on Indiana's guest statute. Paul (P) appealed, contending that West Virginia's lex loci delicti rule of conflicts should be abandoned, and West Virginia's law applied.

ISSUE: Should the doctrine of lex loci delicti be abandoned?

HOLDING AND DECISION: (Neely, J.) No. The doctrine of lex loci delicti should not be abandoned. Beginning in the early 1960s, courts began jettisoning the traditional lex loci rule in favor of more flexible, factor-based analyses of relative governmental interests. The problem with these approaches is that they tend to be so amorphous as to contain no predictability. The lex loci rule, on the other hand, is eminently wieldy and predictable. It appears that most courts abandoned the lex loci rule to avoid application of foreign laws they perceived as unjust, such as guest statutes and interspousal immunity. Today, however, such laws are rare, and their uncommon presence is insufficient to justify abolition of the lex loci rule, which this court considers superior to the governmental interest "rule." [The court went on to hold that, in this case, application of Indiana's guest statute would be contrary to West Virginia public policy, and it reversed.]

EDITOR'S ANALYSIS: The approach taken by the court here is rather singular. Almost every other court that has revisited the lex loci rule in recent years has rejected it. It is interesting to note that, even though the court here retained the rule, it did not follow it.

[For more information on the lex loci rule, see Casenote Law Outline on Conflict of Laws, Chapter 6, § I, The Traditional Method.]

SALAVARRIA v. NATIONAL CAR RENTAL SYSTEM, INC.
705 So.2d 809 (La. App. 4th Dist. 1998).

NATURE OF CASE: Appeal from denied motion for summary judgment in a negligence action.

FACT SUMMARY: Salavarria (P) and the operator of National (D) rental car were in a car collision in Louisiana. National (D) argued that Louisiana, and not Florida, law should apply.

CONCISE RULE OF LAW: When liability is a question of loss distribution and financial protection, and the injured person and the person who caused the injury are domiciled in different states, then when both the injury and the conduct occurred in one of those states, the law of that state is to be used.

FACTS: Salavarria (P) collided with a car owned by National (D). The car had been rented to Brogdon but the driver of the car was Trempe. Trempe was not an authorized driver of the car. Salavarria (P) was a Louisiana resident, and Louisiana was where the accident occurred. Brogdon and Trempe were Florida residents, and the contract was entered into in Florida. National (D) filed a motion for summary judgment arguing Louisiana law applied and that a self-insured car rental agency has the right to restrict the use of rental vehicles to authorized users and, therefore, can't be liable for accidents caused by unauthorized users. The trial court denied the motion, finding that Florida law controlled. Florida doesn't distinguish between authorized and unauthorized users but holds owners vicariously liable. National (D) appealed.

ISSUE: Does Florida or Louisiana law govern?

HOLDING AND DECISION: (Byrnes, J.) Louisiana law governs. The conduct that resulted in Plaintiff's injuries occurred in Louisiana, and Louisiana standard of care must apply. National's (D) liability is a question of loss distribution and financial protection. Louisiana's conflict of law statute states that when parties are domiciled in different states, loss distribution and financial protection are governed by the law of the state where the injury and the conduct that caused it occurred, if one of the parties is domiciled there. Since both the injury and the conduct that caused it occurred in Louisiana, Plaintiff is a Louisiana domiciliary, and Trempe is a Florida resident, Louisiana law should be applied. Since Plaintiff didn't base National's (D) liability on contract but rather on Florida law, Louisiana policies governing loss distribution and financial protection would be seriously impaired by the application of Florida law because the overwhelming preponderance of the contracts out of which this litigation arises are with the state of Louisiana. In addition, the choice is not to be based on the benefit or detriment of the litigants, and Florida policies are not impaired by this decision. Reversed.

EDITOR'S ANALYSIS: In an effort to produce more satisfactory results than common law has produced, legislatures have enacted conflict of law statutes, such as the one discussed in this case.

HOME INSURANCE CO. v. DICK
381 U.S. 397 (1930).

NATURE OF CASE: Review of award of damages for breach of an insurance contract.

FACT SUMMARY: A Texas statute was contended to nullify a contractual limitations period in a contract having no relationship to Texas.

CONCISE RULE OF LAW: A state may not by law nullify a contractual limitations period in a contract having no relationship to that state.

FACTS: Dick (P) entered into an insurance contract with a Mexican insurance company to cover a certain boat. The agreement was negotiated in Mexico. By agreement with the Mexican insurer, Home Insurance Co. (D) and Franklin Fire Insurance Co. (D), both New York corporations, provided reinsurance services. The boat was lost, and the Mexican insurer never paid. Dick (P) brought an action in Texas state court against Home (D) and Franklin (D). They asserted as a defense a clause in the contract providing that any action on the contract had to be brought within one year of the qualifying loss. Dick (P) countered by invoking Article 5545 of Texas' Civil Statutes, which provided that no contractual limitations period could be less than two years. The trial court awarded damages, and this was affirmed on appeal. The Supreme Court granted certiorari.

ISSUE: May a state by law nullify a contractual limitations period in a contract having no relationship to that state?

HOLDING AND DECISION: (Brandeis, J.) No. A state may not by law nullify a contractual limitations period in a contract having no relationship to that state. A state may prohibit and declare invalid as against public policy the making of certain contracts within its borders. Also, it may prohibit performance within its borders of contracts created elsewhere. However, a state may not, consistent with due process, invalidate a portion of a contract made elsewhere and to be performed elsewhere solely by virtue of the fact an action is brought there. In short, a state may not abrogate the rights of persons outside its borders and having no relation to the state. Here, the contract was made in Mexico, and the only relation Texas had to the contract was its status as forum state. This is insufficient to allow its statute to be applicable against non-Texas defendants. Reversed.

EDITOR'S ANALYSIS: The two main constitutional limitations on choice of law are the Due Process and Full Faith and Credit Clauses. Courts are sometimes analytically sloppy about which clause is to be applied to any given situation. This can be significant, as the scope of the clauses do differ. For instance, the Full Faith and Credit Clause is inapplicable to foreign states, while Due Process is not.

[For more information on due process, see Casenote Law Outline on Conflict of Laws, Chapter 3, § II, The Due Process Clause.]

NOTES:

PACIFIC EMPLOYERS INSURANCE CO. v.
INDUSTRIAL ACCIDENT COMMISSION
306 U.S. 493 (1939).

NATURE OF CASE: Appeal from award of workmen's compensation benefits.

FACT SUMMARY: The claimant was a Massachusetts employee of a Massachusetts employer who was injured while on the job in California. He filed a claim for benefits under the California Workmen's Compensation Act.

CONCISE RULE OF LAW: The full faith and credit doctrine may not be invoked where the strong public policy of the forum state would find the enforcement of another state's statutes obnoxious.

FACTS: While in California on company business, a Massachusetts employee of a Massachusetts employer was injured in the course of his duties. He filed a claim for benefits under the California Workmen's Compensation Act and was granted the benefits provided by the California Act. The Industrial Accident Commission of California (P) directed that the claimant's benefits be paid by Pacific Employers Insurance Co. (D), the employer's insurance carrier. The company contended that benefits should be awarded on the basis of benefits provided by the Massachusetts workmen's compensation laws, since the contract of employment was entered into in Massachusetts. The Massachusetts statutes setting forth the jurisdiction over compensable injuries stated that the employee waived his rights to recover under the laws of another state unless he specifically gave written notice of an election not to waive. The claimant gave no such notice. The applicable California statute provided that California would have exclusive jurisdiction over accidents occurring within the state. Both statutes gave the respective states jurisdiction over injuries outside the state where the contract of hire was entered into within the state. Pacific Employers (D) contended that the Full Faith and Credit Clause required California to recognize the provisions of the Massachusetts Act.

ISSUE: Does the Full Faith and Credit Clause require a forum state to enforce the laws of another state despite a strong public policy in the forum state to control accidents within its borders?

HOLDING AND DECISION: (Stone, J.) No. The Massachusetts statutes vesting jurisdiction in that state over accidents occurring within that state under a contract of hire entered into in Massachusetts is certainly constitutional. The same may be said of the similar California provisions. Each state could voluntarily opt to enforce the statutes of the other in appropriate circumstances. Each state has a valid interest in providing for the welfare of its own employees injured within the state and may provide for the compensation of employees temporarily out of state. But to force California to enforce the Massachusetts provisions would be to deny to California the right to give effect to the strong public policy of that state rightfully translated into law. The employee was injured in California, his benefits are payable there, and any medical bills or other attendant expenses will be incurred there. To enforce full faith and credit would be to deny to California the right to apply its own remedy and it would be administratively difficult, if not impossible, to provide the claimant his remedies provided by Massachusetts. This would leave the claimant without a viable remedy for his injuries. The Full Faith and Credit Clause does not empower one state to legislate for another or to project its own laws across state lines where to do so would offend the public policy of the other state. Affirmed.

EDITOR'S ANALYSIS: This case is an example of the development of choice of law rules in rejection of the vested rights doctrine. While couched in a full faith and credit context, the real issue in this case was choice of law and due process. The Supreme Court has generally followed the policy of enforcing full faith and credit only in those situations where the state having jurisdiction over the parties has asserted its law. This case represents a choice of laws analysis based on the most significant contact theory. Under this theory, the court looks at the conduct of the parties and the location where that conduct occurred. The court then determines which activities are relevant to the issues of the lawsuit and where those relevant activities occurred. The state in which the most number of significant or relevant contacts were made concerning the transaction is deemed to have the most appropriate law to apply. While this approach might appear to be somewhat mechanical, in operation it becomes rather discretionary. The determination of which activities are significant is not a scientific process. Further, the court may decide that one significant contact is more relevant than another. In this case, the place of contracting for the employment was a significant contact with Massachusetts. But the California court found that the place of contracting had little relevance and, consequently, gave that contact little weight in its decision. Critics of this approach have pointed to this as a defect in the application of the significant contact approach. They argue that while the contact analysis may be a more realistic approach to choice of laws than was the vested right doctrine, the wide discretion given to the court leads to a loss of uniformity and predictability of result.

[For more information on public policy and full faith and credit, see Casenote Law Outline on Conflict of Laws, Chapter 3, § III, The Full Faith and Credit Clause.]

WATSON v. EMPLOYERS LIABILITY ASSURANCE CORP.
348 U.S. 66 (1954).

NATURE OF CASE: Review of dismissal of action for damages for personal injury.

FACT SUMMARY: Watson (P) sought to bring a direct action against an out-of-state insurance company on account of an accident which occurred in her home state of Louisiana, an act permitted locally but not in the insurer's home state.

CONCISE RULE OF LAW: A state may apply its own law against foreign defendants in suits based on injuries that occurred within that state.

FACTS: Employers Liability Assurance Corp. (D), a Massachusetts insurer, insured the maker of a home permanent kit. The insurance contract was negotiated in Massachusetts and Illinois. Watson (P), a Louisiana resident, purchased a kit in Louisiana and attempted to use it there, suffering personal injuries. Louisiana law permitted direct actions against a tortfeasor's insurer, while Massachusetts and Illinois law did not. Watson (P) filed a state court action in Louisiana against Employers (D), seeking damages. Employers (D) removed the case to federal court and moved to dismiss, contending that Louisiana could not constitutionally impose its direct action law on a nonresident carrier for an insurance contract not executed there. The district court agreed and dismissed. The court of appeals affirmed, and the Supreme Court granted review.

ISSUE: May a state apply its own law against foreign defendants in suits based on injuries that occurred within that state?

HOLDING AND DECISION: (Black, J.) Yes. A state may apply its own law against foreign defendants in suits based on injuries that occurred within that state. A state may not, consistent with due process, attempt to impose its laws on a party having no connection with that state. However, to the extent that that foreign defendant is connected with the state, the state may regulate the defendant. Here, the insurance contract between Employers (D) and the manufacturer of the product in question had an impact upon Louisiana in that the kit was purchased and used there. Louisiana has an interest in seeing to it that its injured citizens are adequately compensated, and its direct action law is an expression thereof. Since Employers (D) created an effect in Louisiana by insuring a product sold there, Louisiana may employ its direct action law. Reversed.

CONCURRENCE: (Frankfurter, J.) Louisiana could, as a condition of doing business there, require Employers (D) to accept its direct action law. This nonconstitutional ground would be a better basis for a decision than the constitutional grounds discussed by the Court.

EDITOR'S ANALYSIS: The Fourteenth Amendment's Due Process Clause places limits on the extraterritorial reach of state law respecting out-of-state defendants. This relates both to personal jurisdiction and choice of law. A state may not alter the terms of out-of-state contracts with which the state has no connection. Here, however, Employers (D) had entered the state by insuring a product there.

[For more information on due process, see Casenote Law Outline on Conflict of Laws, Chapter 3, § II, The Due Process Clause.]

NOTES:

63

CLAY v. SUN INSURANCE OFFICE LTD.
377 U.S. 179 (1964).

NATURE OF CASE: Suit against an insurance company on a casualty insurance policy.

FACT SUMMARY: Clay (P) purchased an insurance policy in Illinois and subsequently moved to Florida. A loss occurred and a suit resulted that was barred by the policy provisions but allowable under Florida law.

CONCISE RULE OF LAW: Where suit is brought on an ambulatory contract executed in a state other than the forum, the forum state is not obliged to substitute a conflicting out-of-state statute for its own statute.

FACTS: While a resident of Illinois, Clay (P) purchased a policy of insurance on his personal property from Sun Insurance (D). A provision of the policy barred suits arising out of claims against the company brought more than 12 months after denial of the claim. This provision was permissible under Illinois law. Clay (P) subsequently moved to Florida, where he resided for two years, returning the policy after the move. He sustained a loss while in Florida. The company denied his claim, and he instituted suit against the company. However, the suit was commenced beyond the 12-month limit of the policy provision. A statute in Florida provided that any clause limiting the time to file suit to less than five years was void. Sun Insurance (D) was licensed to do business in Illinois, Florida, and several other states. Sun Insurance (D) contended that the Full Faith and Credit Clause compelled Florida to give effect to the policy provision which was valid under Illinois law since the policy was executed there. Clay (P) contended that Sun Insurance (D) was subject to the laws of Florida and, since the loss occurred in that state, the Florida statute was controlling.

ISSUE: Where the forum state has jurisdiction over the claim, must it apply the local law of the state where the contract was executed in a suit arising out of that contract?

HOLDING AND DECISION: (Douglas, J.) No. Contracts of insurance on personal property are ambulatory in nature. The place of execution may have no relation to the place of loss of covered property. It was certainly within the contemplation of the parties that suit on this policy could be brought in any of the several states. The policy itself purports to provide worldwide coverage for losses. There was no stipulation in the policy that the law of Illinois would govern disputes arising under the policy. The company was aware of Clay's (P) move to Florida. It did not attempt to cancel the coverage. In fact, Sun Insurance (D) is licensed to do business in Florida. It must have contemplated it could be sued there. Since Florida properly had jurisdiction over this suit, and since the contract was ambulatory in nature, Florida was free to apply its own statute without violating the Full Faith and Credit Clause of the Constitution.

EDITOR'S ANALYSIS: One commentator on this case pointed out that applying a Florida statute to this policy after it had been issued in Illinois and performed there amounted to a form of retroactive application. He felt that such retroactive effect was a constitutionally impermissible denial of due process to the insurance company. However, most views of this case have been favorable in light of the number of contacts existing with Florida. Since the insured had lived in Florida for some time, it would seem incongruous to bind him to a statute in a state where he no longer had any contacts. The insurance company was doing business in Florida, thereby acquiescing to that state's laws, and any policies issued in Florida would be subject to the five-year limitation. By this decision, Clay (P) was placed in an equal position with other Florida residents with similar claims.

[For more information on choice of law and contracts, see Casenote Law Outline on Conflict of Laws, Chapter 7, § II, Some Modern Approaches.]

NOTES:

ALLSTATE INS. CO. v. HAGUE
50 U.S. 101 (1981).

NATURE OF CASE: Action for a declaratory judgment regarding insurance coverage.

FACT SUMMARY: After her husband's death in a Wisconsin accident, Hague (P) moved to Minnesota, where he had been employed, and there sought a declaration that Minnesota law applied and would permit "stacking" of his three $15,000 insurance policies to provide total coverage of $45,000.

CONCISE RULE OF LAW: For a state's substantive law to be selected in a constitutionally permissible manner as applying in a particular case, that state must have a significant contact or significant aggregation of contacts, creating state interests, such that choice of its law is neither arbitrary nor fundamentally unfair.

FACTS: Hague's (P) husband, a Wisconsin resident who commuted to work in Minnesota, died of injuries suffered when a motorcycle on which he was a passenger was struck from behind by an automobile. All those involved were Wisconsin residents. Mrs. Hague (P) subsequently moved to Minnesota and remarried, after which Minnesota appointed her representative of her deceased husband's estate. Thereafter, she brought an action in Minnesota seeking a declaration under Minnesota law that the $15,000 uninsured motorist coverage on each of her late husband's three automobiles could be "stacked" to provide total coverage of $45,000. Allstate (D), which issued the policies, did business in Minnesota but argued that Wisconsin law, which did not permit stacking, should be applied. The district court applied Minnesota law and rendered a judgment for Hague (P), which the Minnesota Supreme Court affirmed. On appeal, the constitutionality of choosing Minnesota law to govern the issue was questioned.

ISSUE: Is selection of a state's law to govern a particular issue constitutionally valid as long as that choice of law is neither arbitrary nor fundamentally unfair?

HOLDING AND DECISION: (Brennan, J.) Yes. The lesson to be learned from prior cases which found insufficient forum contacts to apply forum law is that for a state's substantive law to be selected in a constitutionally permissible manner, that state must have a significant contact or aggregation of contacts, creating state interests, such that choice of its law is neither arbitrary nor fundamentally unfair. In this case, such an aggregation of contacts exists. Hague was employed in Minnesota, Allstate (D) was present and doing business there, and Mrs. Hague (P) had become a resident there prior to instituting this litigation. Thus, application of Minnesota law was permissible. Affirmed.

CONCURRENCE: (Stevens, J.) Although I regard the Minnesota courts' decision to apply forum law as unsound as a matter of conflicts law, our authority may be exercised in the choice-of-law

area only to prevent a violation of the Full Faith and Credit or the Due Process Clause and there were no such violations in this case. First, Allstate (D) failed to establish that Minnesota's refusal to apply Wisconsin law posed any direct or indirect threat to Wisconsin's sovereignty. Second, neither the "stacking" rule itself nor Minnesota's application of that rule to these litigants raised any serious question of fairness.

DISSENT: (Powell, J.) The Court should invalidate a forum state's decision to apply its own law only when there are no significant contacts between the state and the litigation. In this particular case, the Court did not adequately analyze the policies that its review of state choice-of-law decisions under the Constitution must serve. In consequence, it has found significant what appear to be trivial contacts between the forum state and the litigation. A contact, or pattern of contacts, satisfies the Constitution when it protects the litigants from being unfairly surprised if the forum state applies its own law, and when the application of the forum's law reasonably can be understood to further a legitimate public policy of the forum state. The contacts identified in this case are either trivial or irrelevant to the furthering of any public policy of Minnesota.

EDITOR'S ANALYSIS: In many prior cases, the Court had spoken in terms of weighing or balancing the interests of the concerned states in deciding choice-of-law cases under the Full Faith and Credit Clause of the Constitution. However, a footnote in this opinion proclaimed that such balancing "is no longer required."

[For more information on indistinguishability of due process and full faith and credit questions, see Casenote Law Outline on Conflict of Laws, Chapter 3, § I, A Current Overview.]

NOTES:

PHILLIPS PETROLEUM CO. v. SHUTTS
472 U.S. 797 (1985).

NATURE OF CASE: Review of award of damages for breach of contract.

FACT SUMMARY: A Kansas state court applied Kansas law to all parties in a class-action suit, even though a minuscule percentage of the plaintiffs and none of the defendants lived in Kansas.

CONCISE RULE OF LAW: In a class-action suit wherein only a small portion of the parties reside in a state and the subject matter of the suit mostly arose elsewhere, that state cannot apply its own law to the entire litigation.

FACTS: Phillips Petroleum Co. (D), a Delaware corporation, had oil and gas leases with persons in all 50 states. For a period of time, it charged customers higher rates in anticipation of regulatory approval of such rates but did not pass increased royalties along to lessors. Eventually the higher rates were approved. Back royalties were paid, but interest thereon was not. Shutts (P) filed a class-action suit in Kansas state court on behalf of some 33,000 royalty owners for back interest on owed royalties. Only about 3% of the plaintiff class and 1% of covered leases were located in Kansas. The Kansas court, applying Kansas law, held that all royalty owners were entitled to back interest and entered a multimillion-dollar award. Phillips (D) appealed, contending that Kansas law should not have been applied to non-Kansas plaintiffs and leases. The verdict was affirmed on appeal, and the Supreme Court granted review.

ISSUE: In a class-action suit wherein only a small portion of the parties reside in a state and the subject matter of the suit mostly arose elsewhere, may a state apply its own law to the entire litigation?

HOLDING AND DECISION: (Rehnquist, J.) No. In a class-action suit wherein only a small portion of the parties reside in a state and the subject matter of the suit mostly arose elsewhere, that state cannot apply its own law to the entire litigation. For a state's law to be applied to any claim, that state must have a significant contact or aggregation of contacts so as to create a state interest in having its law applied to that claim. To do otherwise would violate due process and full faith and credit, as well as contravene the reasonable expectation of parties who entered into the transaction underlying claims having no relation to the forum state. Even when claims are joined in a class, this rule must be followed, unless the forum can show some kind of common fund existing in the forum touching all claims. Here, Kansas only had an interest in 3% of the plaintiffs and 1% of the leases. The vast majority of leases were entered into without any thought of Kansas law, and it would violate due process and full faith and credit to allow Kansas law to apply to all claims. Reversed.

CONCURRENCE AND DISSENT: (Stevens, J.) As there appears to be no conflict between Kansas law and any other state law regarding the legal issues here, no constitutional violation occurred.

EDITOR'S ANALYSIS: Becoming a plaintiff in a class-action suit does not require any voluntary activity. In most jurisdictions, including the federal courts, once a class is certified, a would-be plaintiff must affirmatively opt out if so desired. Were this not the case, the argument could probably be made that, by becoming a plaintiff, a person in a class obtains a significant contact with the forum state.

[For more information on due process, see Casenote Law Outline on Conflict of Laws, Chapter 3, § II, The Due Process Clause.]

NOTES:

SUN OIL CO. v. WORTMAN
108 S. Ct. 2117 (1988).

NATURE OF CASE: Review of denial of motion to dismiss action for damages for breach of contract.

FACT SUMMARY: Kansas, forum state in a class-action suit involving application of the law of several states, applied its statute of limitations to all claims.

CONCISE RULE OF LAW: A forum state may apply its statute of limitations to claims decided under the law of another state.

FACTS: Sun Oil Co. (D) charged higher rates to customers pending regulatory approval thereof but did not pass increased royalties on to the owners of properties from which oil and gas was extracted. A class-action suit was brought in Kansas on behalf of those holding royalty rights on such properties. Sun Oil (D) moved to dismiss some of the claims, based on the statute of limitations of the various states in which the properties were located. The trial court instead applied Kansas's five-year statute and denied the motion as to most of the claims. The Kansas Supreme Court affirmed, and the Supreme Court granted review.

ISSUE: May a forum state apply its statute of limitations to claims decided under the law of another state?

HOLDING AND DECISION: (Scalia, J.) Yes. A forum state may apply its statute of limitations to claims decided under the law of another state. It has been held long and repeatedly that the Full Faith and Credit Clause of the Constitution does not bar application of the forum state's statute of limitations to claims that substantively arise under the law of another state. This is due to the recognition that a forum state is free to enact its own procedural rules for enforcing rights created under the law of another state, and statutes of limitations have been considered procedural since our nation's inception. Analytically, statutes of limitations are viewed as relating to remedies, not to substantive rights. Consequently, a statute of limitation does not extinguish an underlying right but rather denies a remedy. Nothing in the Constitution prohibits a state from doing this, so Kansas was free to apply its statute in this case. Affirmed.

CONCURRENCE: (Brennan, J.) Statutes of limitations defy characterization as purely substantive or purely procedural, as they contain elements of both. However, they are sufficiently procedural that a forum state has a significant interest in applying its own statute.

CONCURRENCE AND DISSENT: (O'Connor, J.) The result would be more problematic if the jurisdiction whose substantive law is being applied considers its statute of limitations to be procedural.

EDITOR'S ANALYSIS: The present case was a logical successor to Phillips Petroleum Co. v. Shutts, 472 U.S. 797 (1985). That case held in a similar situation involving unpaid royalties that a forum state had to apply the law of the jurisdiction creating the right sued upon. Given this, the issue of competing statutes of limitations was bound to arise.

[For more information on statutes of limitations, see Casenote Law Outline on Conflict of Laws, Chapter 3, § III, The Full Faith and Credit Clause.]

NOTES:

HUGHES v. FETTER
341 U.S. 609 (1951).

NATURE OF CASE: Wrongful death suit.

FACT SUMMARY: Hughes (P), a resident of Illinois, was killed in an auto accident in that state by Fetter (D), a resident of Wisconsin. Hughes' (P) administrator brought a wrongful death suit against Fetter (D) in Wisconsin, although Wisconsin law precluded such suits for deaths outside Wisconsin.

CONCISE RULE OF LAW: While the Full Faith and Credit Clause does not require the forum state to give force to a sister state's law that conflicts with its own public policy, the forum state cannot deny recovery merely because the act giving rise to the lawsuit occurred outside its borders.

FACTS: While Fetter (D) was driving in Illinois, he was involved in an auto accident with Hughes (P). Fetter (D) was a resident of Wisconsin and Hughes (P), who was killed, was a resident of Illinois. Both states had wrongful death statutes and Hughes' (P) administrator brought suit against Fetter (D) in Wisconsin. The suit was dismissed on the ground that the Wisconsin wrongful death statute precluded recovery where the death occurred outside Wisconsin.

ISSUE: May the forum state be required by the Full Faith and Credit Clause to give force to a sister state's law that conflicts with its own public policy?

HOLDING AND DECISION: (Black, J.) No. In this case, however, there is no real conflict. Wisconsin recognizes the wrongful death action, as does Illinois. The only reason for excluding this suit is that the death occurred in Illinois. Since both the defendant individual and the defendant insurance company are domiciled in Wisconsin, there is sufficient contact for Wisconsin to provide a forum. The exclusion cannot be justified on a blanket statutory policy of "forum non conveniens," since in many circumstances Wisconsin might be the only state where jurisdiction could be had over the defendant. While true conflicts in public policies between states must be arbitrated by this court, Wisconsin has no public policy against this type of suit.

DISSENT: (Frankfurter, J.) It is one thing to require a state to respect judgments of other states. It is a very different matter to require them to open their courts to rights of action created by other states but not recognized therein. The Full Faith and Credit Clause does not require such a result.

EDITOR'S ANALYSIS: Some commentators have felt this case was decided on Fourteenth Amendment equal protection grounds, rather than full faith and credit. Application of the similar law in Illinois was later denied enforcement in another suit involving an airplane crash in Utah. The decision was rested on

the same arguments as the principal case. Individual cases of "forum non conveniens" dismissals have been upheld where the facts supported the decision.

[For more information on enforcement of foreign-based rights, see Casenote Law Outline on Conflicts, Chapter 3, § III, Full Faith and Credit Clause.]

NOTES:

WELLS v. SIMONDS ABRASIVE CO.
345 U.S. 514 (1953).

NATURE OF CASE: Suit for wrongful death.

FACT SUMMARY: Wells (P) was killed in Alabama when a grinding wheel manufactured by Simonds (D) in Pennsylvania exploded. Suit was brought in federal court in Pennsylvania within the statutory time limit of the Alabama wrongful death act but beyond the Pennsylvania statutory limit.

CONCISE RULE OF LAW: The Full Faith and Credit Clause does not require the forum state to give effect to a sister state's statute of limitations even though the action sued upon arose under the law of the sister state.

FACTS: Wells was killed by an exploding grinding wheel in Alabama. The wheel was manufactured in Pennsylvania by Simonds (D). Both states had wrongful death statutes, but the Alabama statute provided that suits must be brought within two years of the death while Pennsylvania had a one-year statute. Since valid service could not be had on Simonds (D) in Alabama, Wells' (P) administrator brought suit in federal court in Pennsylvania more than one year, but less than two years, after the death. Summary judgment was granted to Simonds (D).

ISSUE: Where the forum's statute of limitations differs from the limitation imposed by the state where the action arose, must the forum state recognize the other state's limitation rather than its own?

HOLDING AND DECISION: (Vinson, J.) No. This court has consistently held that the Full Faith and Credit Clause does not require the forum state to give force to a sister state's statute of limitations that differs from its own. There is no unequal treatment imposed by this rule since all wrongful death suits in Pennsylvania are subject to the same limitation, whether the death occurred in state or out. The argument is made that since this cause of action was not recognized by the common law, the statute creating the cause of action includes as an inseparable section the limitation imposed by the statute. This is an insufficient reason to grant an exception to the previously stated rule.

DISSENT: (Jackson, J.) The Full Faith and Credit Clause requires that the law of the state where the cause of action arises follow the litigant wherever the action is adjudicated. Since the cause of action arose in Alabama, that state's law should be applied.

EDITOR'S ANALYSIS: The statute of limitations on a cause of action is generally held to be procedural. Procedural law is not entitled to full faith and credit recognition, only substantive law. Under this rationale, if Pennsylvania had the longer statute of limitations, Wells (P) could have recovered in Pennsylvania when he would have been barred in Alabama.

[For more information on even-handed application of forum procedural rules, see Casenote Law Outline on Conflict of Laws, Chapter 3, § III, Full Faith and Credit Clause.]

NOTES:

NEVADA v. HALL
440 U.S. 410 (1979).

NATURE OF CASE: Appeal of denial of motion for remittitur upon award of damages for personal injury.

FACT SUMMARY: Nevada (D), sued in a California court, contended that the court must respect Nevada's (D) statutory limitation on damages.

CONCISE RULE OF LAW: The courts of one state are not obligated to enforce the statutory damage caps of another state when that other state is a defendant.

FACTS: Bell (P) was injured when an employee of Nevada (D) drove a vehicle into his vehicle. The accident occurred in California, where Bell (P) lived. Bell (P) sued Nevada (D) in California state court. The court entered a substantial judgment in favor of Bell (P). Nevada (D) moved for a remittitur, contending that the Full Faith and Credit Clause, as embodying concepts of sovereign immunity, required that California courts respect Nevada's (D) $25,000 cap on personal injury awards against the State (D). The motion was denied, and the California Court of Appeals affirmed. The Supreme Court granted review.

ISSUE: Are the courts of one state obligated to enforce the statutory damage caps of another state when that other state is a defendant?

HOLDING AND DECISION: (Stevens, J.) No. The courts of one state are not obligated to enforce the statutory damage caps of another state when that other state is a defendant. The concept of sovereign immunity, which arose out of the feudal system, is based on the notion that a sovereign, as the source of law, could not be sued under that law without his consent. This makes sense when that sovereign provides access to legal process, which is to say, when it is sued in its own courts. When it is sued in the courts of another sovereign, however, this rationale for sovereign immunity disappears. Constitutionally speaking, the framers thereof were more concerned with suits against states in federal courts, not suits between states. As far as the Full Faith and Credit Clause is concerned, it does require states to give effect to the law of other states in some circumstances. However, the cases decided under the Clause make it clear that no state must give effect to laws contrary to its public policy. When, as here, a state permits unlimited recovery, imposing another state's limitation on recovery would offend its policy. Consequently, that state will not be required under the Full Faith and Credit Clause to apply the limitation. Affirmed.

DISSENT: (Blackmun, J.) The Court has in essence equated, for purposes of suit, states with private individuals. This opens the door to avenues of liability and interstate retaliation that will prove unsettling to our federal system.

DISSENT: (Rehnquist, J.) While the Constitution does not expressly provide for interstate sovereign immunity, it is safe to say that such a concept was a postulate on which the Constitution was built.

EDITOR'S ANALYSIS: The Eleventh Amendment, by its language, would appear to provide a constitutional basis for sovereign immunity between the states. The amendment holds that U.S. courts may not entertain suits against states. However, this Amendment has been riddled with judicially created exceptions and is of little vitality. Relevant to this suit, the Amendment has been held not to apply when a state is a plaintiff.

[For more information on suits between states, see Casenote Law Outline on Conflict of Laws, Chapter 4, § IV, Federal Common Law.]

NOTES:

AUSTIN v. NEW HAMPSHIRE
420 U.S. 656 (1975).

NATURE OF CASE: Review of order dismissing constitutional challenge to state taxation system.

FACT SUMMARY: New Hampshire (D) created a tax system that had the effect of taxing the in-state income of nonresidents only.

CONCISE RULE OF LAW: A state may not impose an income tax on only nonresidents' in-state income.

FACTS: New Hampshire (D) enacted a tax system which, when various offsets and rebates were taken into account, had the effect of taxing in-state income of nonresidents while not taxing in-state income of residents. This system was challenged by Austin (P) as unconstitutional. The state trial and supreme courts upheld the tax law, and the Supreme Court granted review.

ISSUE: May a state impose an income tax on only nonresidents' in-state income?

HOLDING AND DECISION: (Marshall, J.) No. A state may not impose an income tax on only nonresidents' in-state income. The Privileges and Immunities Clause of Article IV, § 2 provides that the citizens of each state shall be entitled to all the privileges and immunities of citizens in the several states. This clause, which was based on a similar provision in the Articles of Confederation, was adopted to prevent the practice of some states of denying to outlanders privileges granted to its citizens. The underlying goal was to promote interstate harmony by preventing situations of interstate retaliation, which could have fragmented the new union. The cases decided since the Constitution's adoption have consistently held that forms of discrimination against a state's nonresidents which present the opportunity for interstate disharmony are not to be allowed. One principle that has been created is that there must be substantial equality of tax treatment between residents and nonresidents. Here, the tax system in question clearly does not provide such substantial equality and, therefore, cannot stand. Reversed.

DISSENT: (Blackmun, J.) The tax framework is such that the legislature of a nonresident's state could, if it so desired, divert the New Hampshire tax to its own coffers. Since sister states can opt their citizens out of the tax, no privileges and immunities issue exists.

EDITOR'S ANALYSIS: The Court did not address the Equal Protection Clause, which was also asserted in this case. That provision has also been used to invalidate discriminatory tax/ spending systems. Probably the most notable example was Zobel v. Williams, 457 U.S. 55 (1982). In that case, the Court struck down an Alaska plan that distributed state oil revenues to Alaska citizens but not its noncitizen residents.

[For more information on the Privileges and Immunities Clause, see Casenote Law Outline on Conflict of Laws, Chapter 3, § IV, Other Constitutional Provisions.]

NOTES:

G.D. SEARLE & CO. v. COHN
455 U.S. 404 (1982).

NATURE OF CASE: Review of order reinstating a dismissed personal injury action.

FACT SUMMARY: Searle & Co. (D) contended that a provision tolling New Jersey's statute of limitations against out-of-state corporate defendants violated equal protection.

CONCISE RULE OF LAW: A state may by law toll the running of its statute of limitations against out-of-state corporate defendants.

FACTS: Cohn (P) suffered a stroke in 1963. In 1974, her husband and she filed suit against G.D. Searle & Co. (D) in New Jersey state court, alleging that medication Cohn (P) had taken had precipitated the stroke. Searle (D) removed the case to U.S. district court and moved to dismiss, citing New Jersey's two-year statute of limitations. The district court granted the motion, rejecting Cohn's (P) contention that running of the statute was tolled against out-of-state defendants without agents in the state. The court held the statute violated equal protection. The court of appeals reversed, and the Supreme Court granted review.

ISSUE: May a state by law toll the running of its statute of limitations against out-of-state corporate defendants?

HOLDING AND DECISION: (Blackmun, J.) Yes. A state may by law toll the running of its statute of limitations against out-of-state corporate defendants. In the absence of a classification that is inherently invidious or that impinges upon a fundamental right, a state may regulate a matter as it sees fit, so long as the classification is rational. A statute of limitations is no fundamental right, and states may provide statutes and exceptions thereto as they see fit. The stated purpose of the exception to the two-year statute is the possibility that out-of-state corporate defendants may be hard to locate and serve if no in-state agents therefor are present. This is a rational conclusion, and the fact that New Jersey has adopted a long-arm statute in no way changes this. Consequently, the tolling provision did not offend the Equal Protection Clause. [The Court remanded the case to the court of appeals for a determination of a Commerce Clause challenge to the law.]

DISSENT: (Stevens, J.) It is not rational to deny the benefit of any statute of limitations to a foreign corporation.

EDITOR'S ANALYSIS: Searle (D) attempted a due process argument as well as the equal protection contentions set forth. Essentially, it argued that the statutory scheme required it to appoint an agent for service of process in all cases, even where International Shoe minimum contacts did not exist. The Court expressly refused to consider this argument, as it was not raised in the courts below.

[For more information on the Equal Protection Clause, see Casenote Law Outline on Conflict of Laws, Chapter 3, § IV, Other Constitutional Provisions.]

NOTES:

BROWN-FORMAN DISTILLERS CORP. v. NEW YORK STATE LIQUOR AUTHORITY
476 U.S. 573 (1986).

NATURE OF CASE: Review of order dismissing action challenging constitutionality of state liquor law.

FACT SUMMARY: New York's statutory regulation prohibiting liquor wholesalers from selling at a price higher than the lowest price charged elsewhere in the United States was challenged under the Commerce Clause.

CONCISE RULE OF LAW: A state may not prohibit a liquor distributor from selling at a price higher than the lowest price charged elsewhere in the United States.

FACTS: New York State adopted a statutory regulatory framework covering distilled liquor. The law provided, among other things, that a liquor wholesaler could not sell its product at a price higher than the lowest price charged anywhere else in the United States. This law was challenged by Brown-Forman Distillers Corp. (P) as violating the Commerce Clause. [The casebook opinion did not state whether it was filed in federal or state court.] The lower court upheld the law's validity, and the Supreme Court granted review.

ISSUE: May a state prohibit a liquor distributor from selling at a price higher than the lowest price charged elsewhere in the United States?

HOLDING AND DECISION: (Marshall, J.) No. A state may not prohibit a liquor distributor from selling at a price higher than the lowest price charged elsewhere in the United States. A state may not enact a law that regulates interstate commerce; the Commerce Clause leaves this authority exclusively to Congress. When a state law has extraterritorial effects that amount to regulation of commerce in other states, the law is invalid. When a state mandates that a product can be sold in that state at a price no higher than the lowest price charged in any other state, that state has reserved to itself a veto power over pricing throughout the whole nation, in effect regulating prices nationwide. This is beyond the authority of the states. New York's liquor law is therefore violative of the Commerce Clause. Reversed.

EDITOR'S ANALYSIS: The Court upheld a similar law in Joseph E. Seagram & Sons, Inc. v. Hostetter, 384 U.S. 35 (1966). In that case, an earlier New York law that set prices at the previous month's level was held not to offend the Commerce Clause. In a footnote in the present opinion, the Court cautioned that it was expressing no opinion on the continuing vitality of Seagram as precedent.

[For more information on the Commerce Clause, see Casenote Law Outline on Conflict of Laws, Chapter 3, § IV, Other Constitutional Provisions.]

NOTES:

CTS CORP. v. DYNAMICS CORPORATION OF AMERICA
481 U.S. 69 (1987).

NATURE OF CASE: Review of order invalidating state corporate takeover restrictions.

FACT SUMMARY: Indiana enacted a law which required, prior to acquisition of specified levels of control in its corporations, majority approval of the target corporation's shareholders.

CONCISE RULE OF LAW: A state may require, for one of its corporations to be acquired, majority approval of the target's shareholders.

FACTS: Indiana enacted what it called the Control Share Acquisitions Act, a law applying to corporations having significant contacts with the state, such as being incorporated there or having more than 10% of its shares held by Indiana residents. The law required that, prior to any acquisition of 20%, 33 %, or 50% control in the corporation, the tender offeror needed to obtain approval of a majority of shareholders. In 1986, Dynamics Corporation of America (P), holder of 9.6% of stock in CTS Corp. (D), an Indiana corporation, announced a tender offer for 27.5% control. It soon thereafter filed suit in federal district court, contending that the state statute violated the Williams Act and the Commerce Clause. The district court struck down the law on both grounds, and the Seventh Circuit affirmed. The Supreme Court granted review.

ISSUE: May a state require, for one of its corporations to be acquired, majority approval of the target's shareholders?

HOLDING AND DECISION: (Powell, J.) Yes. A state may require, for one of its corporations to be acquired, majority approval of the target's shareholders. [The casebook opinion omitted the Court's discussion of the Williams Act and went directly into the Court's Commerce Clause analysis.] The dormant Commerce Clause principally deals with attempts by states either to discriminate against or to regulate interstate commerce, or with laws that carry the likelihood of subjecting goods or services to inconsistent regulations. A law such as that enacted by Indiana here does none of these. The law deals with Indiana corporations only. It treats out-of-state tender offerors the same as Indiana tender offerors and does not purport to regulate out-of-state corporations. Corporations are creatures of state law, and states have broad powers to regulate them. While it is true that the law in question may discourage tender offers, which is an economically questionable goal, it is not the role of this Court to impose any particular economic theory on the states. So long as the minimum requirements of the Commerce Clause are met, as they have been here, states may regulate their corporations as they see fit. Reversed.

CONCURRENCE: (Scalia, J.) Once it is established that a law neither discriminates against interstate commerce nor places an undue risk of inconsistent regulation, no further discussion is necessary.

DISSENT: (White, J.) The law applies to stock traded in interstate commerce (here the New York Stock Exchange) and, as such, regulates interstate commerce.

EDITOR'S ANALYSIS: The Williams Act, discussion of which was omitted here, is the federal regulation of tender offers. The Act provides for certain reporting requirements when a tender offer is made. In the portions edited from the case here, the Court concluded that the Williams Act was concerned with disclosure and did not affect attempts by states to alter the balance of power between shareholders and acquirers.

[For more information on the Commerce Clause, see Casenote Law Outline on Conflict of Laws, Chapter 3, § IV, Other Constitutional Provisions.]

NOTES:

THE BREMEN v. ZAPATA OFF-SHORE CO.
407 U.S. 1 (1972).

NATURE OF CASE: Review of order denying motion to dismiss action for damages for injury to property.

FACT SUMMARY: A district court held a forum-selection clause in an international contract to be presumptively invalid.

CONCISE RULE OF LAW: A forum-selection clause in a contract of international scope is presumptively valid.

FACTS: Zapata Off-Shore Co. (P) contracted with Unterweser (D), a German corporation, for the latter to tow an offshore oil rig from United States coastal waters to Italian coastal waters. The contract contained a clause giving exclusive jurisdiction over disputes arising out of the contract to English courts. The rig was damaged in transit. Zapata (P) filed an action in U.S. district court, seeking reimbursement for its property damage. Unterweser (D) filed a motion to dismiss, invoking the forum-selection clause. The district court denied the motion, holding such agreements presumptively invalid as contrary to public policy. The Fifth Circuit affirmed en banc, and the Supreme Court granted review.

ISSUE: Is a forum-selection clause in a contract of international scope presumptively valid?

HOLDING AND DECISION: (Burger, C.J.) Yes. A forum-selection clause in a contract of international scope is presumptively valid. The barriers of distance that once made business a matter of local concern no longer exist. The position of American business in international commerce will hardly be helped if courts insist on the parochial concept that trade disputes involving American concerns must be litigated here. We cannot have trade in world markets effected exclusively on our terms and resolved in our courts. Beyond this, the bias against forum-selection clauses reflects an unwillingness to recognize the legitimacy of foreign courts, which is a view that should not be encouraged. The better rule is that forum-selection clauses in contracts are prima facie valid and will be enforced unless shown to be unreasonable. Here, the clause was agreed upon in arms-length negotiations, and there is no evidence that English courts are incompetent to hear the dispute in issue. For these reasons, the forum-selection clause should be enforced. Reversed.

DISSENT: (Douglas, J.) The litigation has much more of a connection with the United States than England, and the matter is, therefore, more appropriately litigated in the United States.

EDITOR'S ANALYSIS: The opinion did not say what would make enforcement of a forum-selection clause unreasonable. Presumably, either incompetence or bias on the part of the selected forum would do so. Also, it is likely that a position of substantially unequal bargaining power would also bring such a clause into question.

[For more information on forum selection, see Casenote Law Outline on Conflict of Laws, Chapter 7, § I, The Traditional Approaches.]

NOTES:

CARNIVAL CRUISE LINES, INC. v. SHUTE
499 U.S. 585 (1991).

NATURE OF CASE: Review of order denying enforcement of a forum-selection clause.

FACT SUMMARY: Mr. and Mrs. Shute (P) of Washington State sued Carnival Cruise Lines (D), headquartered in Miami, Florida, for negligence in federal court in Washington State, and Carnival (D) moved to dismiss the action based on a forum-selection clause in the tickets that required all disputes to be litigated in Florida.

CONCISE RULE OF LAW: A nonnegotiated forum-selection clause in a form contract is enforceable.

FACTS: Mr. and Mrs. Shute (P), residents of Washington State, purchased passenger tickets for a cruise on a ship owned by Carnival Cruise Lines, Inc. (D), which had its headquarters in Miami, Florida. The Shutes (P) bought their tickets through a local travel agent in Washington State. The travel agent forwarded the payment to Carnival (D) in Miami, where the tickets were prepared and then sent to the Shutes (P). On the face of each ticket, in the lower left-hand corner, there was a four-line note advising the ticket-holder that the ticket was subject to the conditions of a contract that appeared on the last pages of the ticket. Paragraph eight of the contract was a provision requiring all disputes arising under the contract to be litigated in courts located in Florida. While the Shutes (P) were aboard Carnival's (D) ship, in international waters off of Mexico, Mrs. Shute (P) was injured when she slipped on a deck mat. The Shutes (P) filed a negligence action against Carnival (D) in the District Court for the Western District of Washington. Carnival (D) moved for summary judgment, contending that the forum clause in the tickets required the Shutes (P) to bring their suit in Florida and, alternatively, that the Washington court lacked personal jurisdiction because of insubstantial contacts. The district court granted Carnival's (D) motion based on lack of personal jurisdiction and the Shutes (P) appealed. The court of appeals reversed, citing Carnival's (D) solicitation of business in Washington, and concluded that the forum clause should not be enforced because it was not freely bargained for. The Supreme Court granted review.

ISSUE: Is a nonnegotiated forum-selection clause in a form contract enforceable?

HOLDING AND DECISION: (Blackmun, J.) Yes. A nonnegotiated forum-selection clause in a form contract is enforceable. The fact that a forum clause is not bargained for is not determinative of its enforceability. Forum-selection clauses contained in form passage contracts are subject to judicial scrutiny for fundamental fairness. In this case, there is no indication that Carnival (D) set Florida as the forum as a means of discouraging cruise passengers from pursuing legitimate claims. Any suggestion of such a bad-faith motive is belied by two facts:

Carnival (D) has its principal place of business in Florida, and many of its cruises depart from and return to Florida ports. Similarly, there is no evidence that Carnival (D) obtained the Shutes' (P) accession to the forum clause by fraud or overreaching. Finally, the Shutes (P) concede that they were given notice of the forum provision; thus, they could have rejected the contract. Reversed and remanded.

DISSENT: (Stevens, J.) Many passengers, like the Shutes (P), do not have a chance to read the forum-selection provision until they have purchased their tickets. But even if passengers received prominent notice of the forum clause before they committed the cost of a cruise, the clause is still unenforceable under traditional principles of federal admiralty law. Courts traditionally have reviewed with heightened scrutiny the terms of contracts of adhesion form contracts offered on a take-or-leave basis by a party with stronger bargaining power. The prevailing rule is still that forum-selection clauses are not enforceable if they were not freely bargained for, create additional expense for one party, or deny one party a remedy.

EDITOR'S ANALYSIS: The Supreme Court is making an economic decision in choosing to enforce the forum clause. There is a savings to be gained, both for litigants and the judiciary, in reducing litigation over motions on appropriate forums for litigation. Further, by allowing Carnival (D) to consent to be sued in Florida on its own terms, consumers benefit from the cheaper fares Carnival (D) can charge as a result of its cost containment.

[For more information on choice-of-forum clauses, see Casenote Law Outline on Conflict of Laws, Chapter 2, § IV, Grounds for Not Exercising Jurisdiction.]

NOTES:

STERNBERG v. O'NEIL
Del. Sup. Ct., 550 A.2d 1105 (1988).

NATURE OF CASE: Appeal of dismissal of shareholder's derivative suit upon motion to quash service of process.

FACT SUMMARY: A Delaware court dismissed GenCorp (D) as not amenable to its jurisdiction, despite appointment of an agent for service of process.

CONCISE RULE OF LAW: A foreign defendant, having appointed an agent for service of process, is amenable to personal jurisdiction.

FACTS: Sternberg (P) filed a shareholder's derivative action against RKO General, Inc. (D), a Delaware corporation, its parent, GenCorp, Inc. (D), an Ohio corporation, and several officers thereof. GenCorp (D) filed a motion to quash service, contending that the court lacked jurisdiction over it. The chancery court held that, despite GenCorp's (D) appointment of an agent for service of process, it lacked minimum contacts with Delaware and was not amenable to suit there. Finding GenCorp (D) to be an indispensable party, the court dismissed the entire action. Sternberg (P) appealed.

ISSUE: Is a foreign defendant, having appointed an agent for service of process, amenable to personal jurisdiction?

HOLDING AND DECISION: (Holland, J.) Yes. A foreign defendant, having appointed an agent for service of process, is amenable to personal jurisdiction. Two independent bases have been recognized by the Supreme Court for the exercise of personal jurisdiction over a nonresident defendant: express consent by appointment of an agent, or implied consent by having minimum contacts with the forum jurisdiction. The two bases are separate and complementary; they are not mutually exclusive. While the Supreme Court has never directly addressed the issue of whether its minimum contacts analysis for implied consent was meant to apply to its previously articulated express consent rule, the cases decided since then appear to presume that it was not. Here, GenCorp (D) expressly consented to jurisdiction by appointing an agent for service of process, so the chancery court's minimum contacts analysis was misplaced. Reversed.

EDITOR'S ANALYSIS: The "express consent" rule was announced by the Supreme Court in Pennsylvania Fire Ins. Co. v. Gold Issue Mining & Milling Co., 243 U.S. 93 (1917). Its minimum contacts analysis was created in International Shoe Co. v. Washington, 326 U.S. 310 (1945). In the years since then, personal jurisdiction jurisprudence has dealt almost exclusively with the latter area; express consent is not usually an issue.

[For more information on personal jurisdiction, see Casenote Law Outline on Conflict of Laws, Chapter 2, § I, Traditional Classifications and Bases.]

NOTES:

PHILLIPS PETROLEUM CO. v. SHUTTS

472 U.S. 797 (1985).

NATURE OF CASE: Review of award of damages for breach of contract.

FACT SUMMARY: Phillips Petroleum (D) contended that class-action plaintiffs had to have minimum contacts with a forum to be included in a litigation.

CONCISE RULE OF LAW: A person need not have minimum contacts with a state to be included as a class-action plaintiff in that state.

FACTS: Phillips Petroleum Co. (D), a Delaware corporation, had oil and gas leases with persons in all 50 states. For a period of time it charged customers higher rates in anticipation of regulatory approval of such rates but did not pass increased royalties along to lessors. Eventually the higher rates were approved. Back royalties were paid, but interest thereon was not. Shutts (P) filed a class-action suit in Kansas state court on behalf of some 33,000 royalty owners for back interest on owed royalties. Only about 3% of the plaintiff class and 1% of covered leases were located in Kansas. The Kansas court, applying Kansas law, held that all royalty owners were entitled to back interest and entered a multimillion dollar award. Phillips (D) appealed, contending that the class should not have been certified as to out-of-state plaintiffs who did not possess minimum contacts with Kansas. The court of appeals affirmed, and the Supreme Court granted review.

ISSUE: Must a person have minimum contacts with a state to be included as a class-action plaintiff in that state?

HOLDING AND DECISION: (Rehnquist, J.) No. A person need not have minimum contacts with a state to be included as a class-action plaintiff in that state. The "minimum contacts" requirement fashioned by this Court is based on the recognition that, because defending a lawsuit in a distant forum constitutes a major burden, due process requires that a person have sufficient contacts with that state such that it would be expected that he have to defend there. Status as a class-action plaintiff is not nearly as vulnerable a position as being a civil defendant. First, a plaintiff class must be certified, so judicial oversight is present. Absent plaintiffs need not worry about adverse judgment, and they are almost never subject to counterclaims or liability for fees or costs. Finally, an absent plaintiff will have, under most state law, the opportunity to opt out of the litigation, an opportunity a civil defendant obviously does not have. For these reasons, due process does not require minimum contacts for absent plaintiffs. [The Court went on to reverse on other grounds.]

EDITOR'S ANALYSIS: It would appear that the rule laid down by the Court would prevail in most circumstances but not necessarily all. Procedural rules for class-action suits do vary among the states; some could conceivably not provide the protections that the Court found to be acceptable substitutes for minimum contacts. For instance, a failure to provide the opt-out opportunity might run afoul of due process.

[For more information on due process, see Casenote Law Outline on Conflict of Laws, Chapter 2, § III, Notice.]

NOTES:

INSURANCE CORPORATION OF IRELAND v. COMPAGNIE DES BAUXITES DE GUINEE

456 U.S. 694 (1982).

NATURE OF CASE: Review of order establishing personal jurisdiction in a breach of contract.

FACT SUMMARY: As a sanction for failure to comply with preappearance discovery, a district court entered an order establishing personal jurisdiction.

CONCISE RULE OF LAW: Personal jurisdiction may be established via a discovery sanction under Fed. R. Civ. P. 37(b).

FACTS: Compagnie des Bauxites de Guinee (P) purchased certain insurance services against business interruptions. Insurance Corporation of Ireland (D) was one such insurer. At one point CBG (P) made a claim, which ICI (D) refused to honor. CBG (P) brought an action in U.S. district court, seeking damages for breach of the insurance contract. ICI (D) contested jurisdiction. The court permitted certain discovery to ascertain jurisdiction. ICI (D) refused to answer the discovery. The court issued an order under Fed. R. Civ. P. 37(b), finding personal jurisdiction to be present. The Supreme Court granted review.

ISSUE: May personal jurisdiction be established via a discovery sanction under Fed. R. Civ. P. 37(b)?

HOLDING AND DECISION: (White, J.) Yes. Personal jurisdiction may be established via a discovery sanction under Fed. R. Civ. P. 37(b). Unlike subject-matter jurisdiction, personal jurisdiction does not relate to the power of a court to hear a case. Personal jurisdiction is a due process limitation, and so long as due process is not offended, personal jurisdiction may be established. Moreover, such jurisdiction is a personal right that may be implicitly or expressly waived. The expression of legal rights may be subject to procedural rules which, if not followed, results in a waiver of those rights. For example, a failure to raise timely personal jurisdiction on an issue constitutes a waiver. So too, it seems to this Court, may a refusal to respond to discovery lead to a Rule 37(b) sanction without offending due process. Here, ICI (D) submitted to the court's jurisdiction for the limited purpose of challenging jurisdiction. Having done so, it was required to comply with discovery orders. Having failed to do so, it waived its jurisdictional objections. Affirmed.

CONCURRENCE: (Powell, J.) In a diversity case, jurisdiction must be established by recourse to state law. This requires a minimum contacts analysis. To the extent a Rule 37(b) sanction would attempt to find jurisdiction without such contacts, serious constitutional problems arise.

EDITOR'S ANALYSIS: There are two basic avenues for contesting jurisdiction. The first is to do what ICI (D) did here, make a special appearance. The second is to default, and then make a collateral attack whenever the plaintiff seeks to enforce the default judgment. The Court's analysis here would appear to apply only to the special appearance option.

[For more information on establishing judicial jurisdiction, see Casenote Law Outline on Conflict of Laws, Chapter 2, § II, The International Shoe Standards.]

NOTES:

HELICOPTEROS NACIONALES DE COLUMBIA, S.A.
v. HALL
466 U.S. 408 (1984).

NATURE OF CASE: Appeal from award of damages for wrongful death.

FACT SUMMARY: Helicopteros (D) (Helicol) contended the Texas courts lacked personal jurisdiction over it due to a lack of minimum contacts with the state.

CONCISE RULE OF LAW: A defendant's contacts with the forum state must constitute continuous and systematic general business contacts in order for the forum state to exercise personal jurisdiction over it.

FACTS: Helicol (D), a Columbian corporation with a principal place of business in Bogota, owned a helicopter which crashed in Peru, killing several U.S. citizens. The citizens were employees of a joint venture headquartered in Texas. Hall (P) and other heirs of the employees sued for wrongful death in Texas state court. Helicol (D) moved to dismiss, contending the Texas court lacked personal jurisdiction over it. The trial court denied the motion, and the jury found against Helicol (D). The court of appeals reversed, holding that Helicol's (D) contacts with Texas, essentially the attendance by a Helicol (D) executive at one meeting in Houston and the purchasing of helicopters and parts in Ft. Worth, were insufficient to constitute the requisite minimum contacts. The Texas Supreme Court reversed, and Helicol (D) appealed.

ISSUE: Do a defendant's contacts with the forum state have to constitute continuous and systematic general business contacts to allow for personal jurisdiction?

HOLDING AND DECISION: (Blackmun, J.) Yes. A defendant's contacts with the forum state must constitute continuous and systematic general business contacts in order for the forum state to exercise personal jurisdiction. It has long been held that purchases and occasional trips to the forum will not, standing alone, establish the requisite minimum contacts. Therefore, because no further showing was made concerning the contacts, the Texas courts lacked personal jurisdiction. Reversed.

DISSENT: (Brennan, J.) The Court improperly focuses on general jurisdiction, without giving sufficient attention to the activities of Helicol (D) as they relate to the subject matter of this lawsuit.

EDITOR'S ANALYSIS: The dissent points out that while the contacts involved may not support general personal jurisdiction, if the particular claim arises out of such contacts, jurisdiction over such claim may exist. The purchases in Ft. Worth were arguably related to the wrongful death claim as they were purchases of helicopter parts, some of which may have been used in the ill-fated helicopter.

_____

[For more information on continuous and systematic activities, see Casenote Law Outline on Conflict of Laws, Chapter 2, § II, The International Shoe Standards.]

NOTES:

BURNHAM v. SUPERIOR COURT OF CALIFORNIA
495 U.S. 604 (1990).

NATURE OF CASE: Review of denial of motion to quash service of process for lack of personal jurisdiction.

FACT SUMMARY: Mr. Burnham (D), a resident of New Jersey who was on a business trip to California when he stopped off to visit with his children and was served with process in Mrs. Burnham's (P) divorce action, contested personal jurisdiction based on a lack of minimum contacts with California.

CONCISE RULE OF LAW: A state court may exercise personal jurisdiction over a nonresident in a suit unrelated to his activities in that state if he is personally served with process while temporarily in that state.

FACTS: Mrs. Burnham (P) and Mr. Burnham (D) separated while living in New Jersey. The couple agreed that Mrs. Burnham (P) would have custody of their two children. Mrs. Burnham (P) moved to California with the two children, where the couple had agreed she would file for divorce on grounds of irreconcilable differences. However, Mr. Burnham (D) subsequently refused to submit to a divorce on those grounds. Mrs. Burnham (P) filed suit for divorce in California anyway. Three weeks later, Mr. Burnham (D) visited southern California on business and then traveled to northern California to see his children. He was served with a California court summons and a copy of Mrs. Burnham's (P) divorce petition when he returned one of the children to Mrs. Burnham's (P) home following a weekend visitation. Later, Mr. Burnham (D) made a special appearance in California Superior Court to contest personal jurisdiction based on a lack of "minimum contacts" with the state. The superior court denied Mr. Burnham's (D) motion to quash service of summons, and the court of appeal denied mandamus relief. The Supreme Court granted review.

ISSUE: May a state court exercise personal jurisdiction over a nonresident in a suit unrelated to his activities in that state if he is personally served with process while temporarily in that state?

HOLDING AND DECISION: (Scalia, J.) Yes. A state court may exercise personal jurisdiction over a nonresident in a suit unrelated to his activities in that state if he is personally served with process while temporarily in that state. Among the most firmly established principles of personal jurisdiction in American tradition is that the courts of a state have jurisdiction over nonresidents who are physically present in the state. Mr. Burnham's (D) contention that, in the absence of "continuous and systematic" contacts with the forum, a nonresident defendant can be subjected to judgment only as to matters that arise out of or relate to his contacts with the forum is based on a misunderstanding of our previous decisions. The test of "minimum contacts" is employed only when examining a state court's exercise of jurisdiction over an absent defendant. Jurisdiction based on physical presence alone constitutes due process because it is one of the continuing traditions of our legal system that define the due process standard of "traditional notions of fair play and substantial justice." Affirmed.

CONCURRENCE: (White, J.) There has been no showing that, as a general proposition, the rule allowing jurisdiction to be obtained over a nonresident by personal service in the forum state is so arbitrary that it should be held violative of due process in every case. Until such a showing is made, claims in individual cases should not be entertained. Otherwise, there will be endless fact-specific litigation.

CONCURRENCE: (Brennan, J.) Every assertion of state-court jurisdiction, even one pursuant to a "traditional" rule such as transient jurisdiction, must comport with contemporary notions of due process. Thus, a minimum-contacts analysis is still necessary. Because a transient defendant actually avails himself of significant benefits provided by the state he visits, and because modern transportation and communications have made it much less burdensome for a party sued to defend himself in a state outside his place of residence, exercise of personal jurisdiction over a defendant based on his voluntary presence in the forum will satisfy due process.

EDITOR'S ANALYSIS: While Justice Brennan objected to Justice Scalia's reliance solely on tradition to validate the exercise of jurisdiction, Justice Scalia was clearly annoyed that Mr. Burnham (D) sought to establish that physical presence in the forum was no longer sufficient to establish jurisdiction. He emphasized that the standard of "traditional notions of fair play and substantial justice" actually developed by analogy to "physical presence."

[For more information on jurisdiction, see Casenote Law Outline on Conflict of Laws, Chapter 2, § I, Traditional Classifications and Bases.]

NOTES:

WORLD-WIDE VOLKSWAGEN CORP. v. WOODSON
444 U.S. 286 (1980).

NATURE OF CASE: Review of denial of petition for writ of prohibition.

FACT SUMMARY: Jurisdiction over an auto distributor was exercised on the basis that one of its autos had entered the state.

CONCISE RULE OF LAW: The fact that a product finds its way into a state is insufficient to confer jurisdiction over its distributor.

FACTS: The Robinsons (P) purchased an Audi from Seaway Volkswagen, Inc. (D), which in turn had obtained it from World-Wide Volkswagen Corp. (D). Seaway (D) was a dealer operating locally in New York; World-Wide (D) was an east coast distributor. Neither did business in Oklahoma. While driving through Oklahoma, the Robinsons (P) were rear-ended. The Robinsons (P) filed suit in Oklahoma state court. Seaway (D) and World-Wide (D) moved to dismiss for lack of personal jurisdiction. The trial court denied the motion. The Oklahoma Supreme Court denied a writ of prohibition, and the Supreme Court granted review.

ISSUE: Will a product finding its way into a state be sufficient to confer jurisdiction over its distributor?

HOLDING AND DECISION: (White, J.) No. The fact that a product finds its way into a state is insufficient to confer jurisdiction over its distributor. It has long been settled that a state may exercise jurisdiction over a person only so long as there are sufficient minimum contacts between the forum and the person such that it would not be unfair to hale him into court there. This is not an expediency that can be dispensed with; due process requires such contacts, even if a state has an otherwise legitimate interest in adjudicating the suit. This is a necessary consequence of our federal system of government. Here, it is clear that such contacts do not exist. In essence, the defendants have done nothing to put themselves within Oklahoma. The fact that it was "foreseeable" that the auto would make its way into Oklahoma does not alter this result. Only when it is foreseeable that a defendant's conduct will make it amenable to a state's jurisdiction will foreseeability be determinative. Such was not the case here. Reversed.

DISSENT: (Brennan, J.) The Court gives insufficient weight to the strength of the forum state's interest in adjudicating the matter and to the inconvenience of the out-of-state defendants.

DISSENT: (Marshall, J.) Because an automobile's utility derives from its mobility, it is not unfair to impose upon an auto's manufacturers/sellers a looser standard of what constitutes due process than most individuals.

EDITOR'S ANALYSIS: In recent years, the Court has begun to take a somewhat more restrictive view of jurisdiction than before. Starting with International Shoe Co. v. Washington, 326 U.S. 310 (1945), the Court gradually relaxed jurisdictional constraints. In the 1970s, the process began to reverse. The present case is an example.

_____

[For more information on jurisdictional requirements, see Casenote Law Outline on Conflict of Laws, Chapter 2, § II, The International Shoe Standards.]

NOTES:

KULKO v. SUPERIOR COURT
436 U.S. 84 (1978).

NATURE OF CASE: Review of denial of motion to quash service in an action seeking increase in child support.

FACT SUMMARY: California courts based jurisdiction over nonresident Kulko (D) on the grounds that he had helped his children to move there.

CONCISE RULE OF LAW: A person is not amenable to a state's jurisdiction merely because he helped his children to move there.

FACTS: Ezra Kulko (D) and Sharon Kulko (later Horn) (P) lived most of their married life in New York. The marriage eventually ended. The parties agreed that their two children would live with Kulko (D) in New York during the school year, and with Horn (P) during summer and Christmas break. Eventually one child expressed an interest in remaining in California. Kulko (D) purchased her a ticket, and she took up residence in California. Kulko's (D) son later did the same, although Horn (P) paid his air fare. Horn (P) filed an action in California Superior Court, seeking an increase in child support. Kulko (D) moved to quash service, contending that California could not exercise jurisdiction over him. The motion was denied. The California Supreme Court affirmed, holding that Kulko's (D) allowing and facilitating his children's relocation to California permitted the assertion of jurisdiction. The Supreme Court granted certiorari.

ISSUE: Is a person amenable to a state's jurisdiction because he helped his children to move there?

HOLDING AND DECISION: (Marshall, J.) No. A person is not amenable to a state's jurisdiction merely because he helped his children to move there. Due process requires that a state may exercise jurisdiction over a person only if he has certain minimum contacts with the state such that haling him into court there would not offend notions of fair play and substantial justice. One form of such contacts is the purposeful availment of the benefits a state has to offer, such as doing business that causes effects within the state. This was the basis upon which the courts below assumed jurisdiction, but was inapplicable to the facts here. Kulko (D) did not cause any "effect" in California. His acquiescence to allowing his children to move to California cannot in any realistic fashion be characterized as purposefully availing himself of benefits in California. To hold otherwise would not only stretch the limits of due process well beyond the breaking point but would discourage civil resolution of custody issues. For these reasons, Kulko (D) cannot be said to have minimum contacts with California. Reversed.

DISSENT: (Brennan, J.) The question here is so close that deference to the courts below is appropriate.

EDITOR'S ANALYSIS: The Kulkos had been married in California in 1959, during a three-day leave Kulko (D) had from his military service. The courts below did not consider this to be a basis for jurisdiction. An argument could be made that this would give California jurisdiction over family law litigation. In brief dicta, the Court indicated that it would have rejected such an argument had it been made.

[For more information on minimum contacts, see Casenote Law Outline on Conflict of Laws, Chapter 2, § II, The International Shoe Standards.]

NOTES:

ASAHI METAL INDUSTRY CO., LTD. v. SUPERIOR COURT OF CALIFORNIA, SOLANO COUNTY
480 U.S. 102 (1987).

NATURE OF CASE: Appeal from discharge of writ quashing service of summons.

FACT SUMMARY: Asahi (P) appealed from a decision of the California Supreme Court discharging a peremptory writ issued by the appeals court quashing service of summons in Cheng Shin's indemnity action, contending that there did not exist minimum contacts between California and Asahi (P) sufficient to sustain jurisdiction.

CONCISE RULE OF LAW: Minimum contacts sufficient to sustain jurisdiction are not satisfied simply by the placement of a product into the stream of commerce coupled with an awareness that its product would reach the forum state.

FACTS: Asahi (P), a Japanese corporation, manufactured tire valve assemblies in Japan, selling some of them to Cheng Shin, a Taiwanese company which incorporated them into the motorcycles it manufactured. Zurcher was seriously injured in a motorcycle accident, and a companion was killed. He sued Cheng Shin, alleging the motorcycle tire manufactured by Cheng Shin was defective. Cheng Shin sought indemnity from Asahi (P), and the main action settled. Asahi (P) moved to quash service of summons, contending that jurisdiction could not be maintained by California, the state in which Zurcher filed his action, consistent with the Due Process Clause of the Fourteenth Amendment. The evidence indicated that Asahi's (P) sales to Cheng Shin took place in Taiwan, and shipments went from Japan to Taiwan. Cheng Shin purchased valve assemblies from other manufacturers. Sales to Cheng Shin never amounted to more than 1.5% of Asahi's (P) income. Approximately 20% of Cheng Shin's sales in the United States are in California. In declaration, an attorney for Cheng Shin stated he made an informal examination of tires in a bike shop in Solano County, where Zurcher was injured, finding approximately 20% of the tires with Asahi's (P) trademark (25% of the tires manufactured by Cheng Shin). The Superior Court (P) denied the motion to quash, finding it reasonable that Asahi (P) defend its claim of defect in their product. The court of appeals issued a peremptory writ commanding the superior court (D) to quash service of summons. The state supreme court reversed and discharged the writ, finding that Asahi's (P) awareness that some of its product would reach California by placing it in the stream of commerce satisfied minimum contacts sufficient to sustain jurisdiction. From this decision, Asahi (P) appealed.

ISSUE: Are minimum contacts sufficient to sustain jurisdiction satisfied by the placement of a product into the stream of commerce, coupled with the awareness that its product would reach the forum state?

HOLDING AND DECISION: (O'Connor, J.) No. Minimum contacts sufficient to sustain jurisdiction are not satisfied by the placement of a product in the stream of commerce, coupled with the awareness that its product would reach the forum state. To satisfy minimum contacts, there must be some act by which the defendant purposefully avails itself of the privilege of conducting activities within the forum state. Although the courts that have squarely addressed this issue have been divided, the better view is that the defendant must do more than place a product in the stream of commerce. The unilateral act of a consumer bringing the product to the forum state is not sufficient. Asahi (P) has not purposefully availed itself of the California market. It does not do business in the state, conduct activities, maintain offices or agents, or advertise. Nor did it have anything to do with Cheng Shin's distribution system, which brought the tire valve assembly to California. Assertion of jurisdiction based on these facts exceeds the limits of due process. [The Court went on to consider the burden of defense on Asahi (P) and the slight interests of the state and Zurcher, finding the assertion of jurisdiction unreasonable and unfair.] Reversed and remanded.

CONCURRENCE: (Brennan, J.) The state supreme court correctly concluded that the stream of commerce theory, without more, has satisfied minimum contacts in most courts which have addressed the issue, and it has been preserved in the decision of this Court.

CONCURRENCE: (Stevens, J.) The minimum contacts analysis is unnecessary; the Court has found by weighing the appropriate factors that jurisdiction under these facts is unreasonable and unfair.

EDITOR'S ANALYSIS: The Brennan concurrence is quite on point in criticizing the plurality for its characterization of this case as involving the act of a consumer in bringing the product within the forum state. The argument presented in World-Wide Volkswagen Corp. v. Woodson, 444 U.S. 286 (1980), cited by the plurality, seems more applicable to distributors and retailers than to manufacturers of component parts.

[For more information on minimum contacts, see Casenote Law Outline on Conflict of Laws, Chapter 2, § II, The International Shoe Standards.]

NOTES:

SHAFFER v. HEITNER
433 U.S. 186 (1977).

NATURE OF CASE: Review of order sequestering certain property pursuant to statute.

FACT SUMMARY: Shaffer (D) contended that property located in Delaware that was unrelated to a suit therein could not automatically be sequestered.

CONCISE RULE OF LAW: Property located in a forum state that is unrelated to a lawsuit cannot automatically be sequestered.

FACTS: Heitner (P) filed a shareholders' derivative action against various officers of Greyhound Corp. (D). The suit was based on a series of events occurring in Oregon. The suit was filed in Delaware Chancery Court. Heitner (P) obtained a writ of sequestration against shares of stock of Greyhound (D) owned by 19 of the defendants in Delaware. Shaffer (D), one of the owners of the sequestered shares, moved to dissolve the sequestration order, contending that the court lacked jurisdiction over both the property and him. The Chancery Court denied the motion, and the Delaware Supreme Court affirmed. The Supreme Court granted review.

ISSUE: May property located in a forum state that is unrelated to a lawsuit automatically be sequestered?

HOLDING AND DECISION: (Marshall, J.) No. Property located in a forum state that is unrelated to a lawsuit cannot automatically be sequestered. Jurisdiction over a thing is, in reality, jurisdiction over the interests of a person in a thing. Consequently, due process considerations exist in a state's exercise of jurisdiction over property, just as they exist in the exercise of jurisdiction over a person. This Court has already established the due process standard of minimum contacts for jurisdiction over a person; it makes great sense to impose the same standard for jurisdiction over the interests in persons over a thing. To hold otherwise would allow a state to obtain jurisdiction over a person indirectly (by forcing him to come to the state to protect his interest in his property) when it could not do so directly. The main argument against imposing a minimum contacts test for actions against property is that not doing so assures the plaintiff of a forum. However, the same could be said as an argument against minimum contacts in in personam jurisdiction. This argument fails under due process. Consequently, for an action against property to lie, minimum contacts must exist. Here, the property in question had nothing to do with the present action, so minimum contacts are not present. The sequestration order was, therefore, invalid. Reversed.

CONCURRENCE: (Powell, J.) The ownership of some forms of property in a state may, in and of itself, confer jurisdiction over the defendant up to the value of the property.

CONCURRENCE: (Stevens, J.) The Delaware sequestration statute is unusually onerous upon a nonresident defendant. It is unclear whether the Court's analysis here should be applied to the sequestration/attachment systems of other states.

CONCURRENCE AND DISSENT: (Brennan, J.) When a corporation is incorporated in a certain state, minimum contacts between that state and its officers and shareholders do exist.

EDITOR'S ANALYSIS: The type of jurisdiction that was at issue above is what is known as quasi in rem. This refers to jurisdiction over property in a suit not concerning the property itself, but rather the owner of the property. This type of jurisdiction was first recognized in Harris v. Balk, 198 U.S. 215 (1905). The present case largely, although not entirely, did away with quasi-in-rem jurisdiction.

_____

[For more information on quasi-in-rem jurisdiction, see Casenote Law Outline on Conflict of Laws, Chapter 2, § I, Traditional Classifications and Bases.]

NOTES:

STERNBERG v. O'NEIL
Del. Sup. Ct., 550 A.2d 1105 (1988).

NATURE OF CASE: Appeal of dismissal of shareholder's derivative suit upon motion to quash service of process.

FACT SUMMARY: A Delaware court dismissed GenCorp (D) as not amenable to its jurisdiction, despite appointment of an agent for service of process.

CONCISE RULE OF LAW: A foreign defendant, having appointed an agent for service of process, is amenable to personal jurisdiction.

FACTS: Sternberg (P) filed a shareholder's derivative action against RKO General, Inc. (D), a Delaware corporation, its parent, GenCorp, Inc. (D), an Ohio corporation, and several officers thereof. GenCorp (D) filed a motion to quash service, contending that the court lacked jurisdiction over it. The chancery court held that, despite GenCorp's (D) appointment of an agent for service of process, it lacked minimum contacts with Delaware and was not amenable to suit there. Finding GenCorp (D) to be an indispensable party, the court dismissed the entire action. Sternberg (P) appealed.

ISSUE: Is a foreign defendant, having appointed an agent for service of process, amenable to personal jurisdiction?

HOLDING AND DECISION: (Holland, J.) Yes. A foreign defendant, having appointed an agent for service of process, is amenable to personal jurisdiction. Two independent bases have been recognized by the Supreme Court for the exercise of personal jurisdiction over a nonresident defendant: express consent by appointment of an agent, or implied consent by having minimum contacts with the forum jurisdiction. The two bases are separate and complimentary; they are not mutually exclusive. While the Supreme Court has never directly addressed the issue of whether its minimum contacts analysis for implied consent was meant to apply to its previously articulated express consent rule, the cases decided since then appear to presume that it was not. Here, GenCorp (D) expressly consented to jurisdiction by appointing an agent for service of process, so the chancery court's minimum contacts analysis was misplaced. Reversed.

EDITOR'S ANALYSIS: The "express consent" rule was announced by the Supreme Court in Pennsylvania Fire Ins. Co. v. Gold Issue Mining & Milling Co., 243 U.S. 93 (1917). Its minimum contacts analysis was created in International Shoe Co. v. Washington, 326 U.S. 310 (1945). In the years since then, personal jurisdiction jurisprudence has dealt almost exclusively with the latter area; express consent is not usually an issue.

[For more information on personal jurisdiction, see Casenote Law Outline on Conflict of Laws, Chapter 2, § I, Traditional Classifications and Bases.]

NOTES:

ERIE RAILROAD CO. v. TOMPKINS
304 U.S. 64 (1938).

NATURE OF CASE: Action to recover damages for personal injury allegedly caused by negligent conduct.

FACT SUMMARY: In a personal injury suit, federal district court trial judge refused to apply applicable state law because such law was "general" (judge-made) and not embodied in any statute.

CONCISE RULE OF LAW: Although the 1789 Rules of Decision Act left federal courts unfettered to apply their own rules of procedure in common-law actions brought in federal court, state law governs substantive issues. State law includes not only statutory law, but case law as well.

FACTS: Tompkins (P) was walking in a right of way parallel to some railroad tracks when an Erie Railroad (D) train came by. Tompkins (P) was struck and injured by what he would, at trial, claim to be an open door extending from one of the rail cars. Under Pennsylvania case law (the applicable law since the accident occurred there), state courts would have treated Tompkins (P) as a trespasser in denying him recovery for other than wanton or willful misconduct on Erie's (b) part. Under "general" law, recognized in federal courts, Tompkins (P) would have been regarded as a licensee and would only have been obligated to show ordinary negligence. Because Erie (D) was a New York corporation, Tompkins (P) brought suit in a federal district court in New York, where he won a judgment for $30,000. Upon appeal to a Federal Circuit Court, the decision was affirmed.

ISSUE: Was the trial court in error in refusing to recognize state case law as the proper rule of decision in deciding the substantive issue of liability?

HOLDING AND DECISION: (Brandeis, J.) Yes. The court's opinion is in four parts: (1) Swift v. Tyson, 41 U.S. (16 Pet.) 1 (1842), which held that federal courts exercising jurisdiction on the ground of diversity of citizenship need not, in matters of general jurisprudence, apply the unwritten law of the state as declared by its highest court, is overruled. Section 34 of the Federal Judiciary Act of 1789, c. 20, 28 U.S. § 725 requires that federal courts in all matters except those where some federal law is controlling, apply as their rules of decision the law of the state, unwritten as well as written. Up to this time, federal courts had assumed the power to make "general law" decisions even though Congress was powerless to enact "general law" statutes; (2) Swift had numerous political and social defects. The hoped-for uniformity among state courts had not occurred; there was no satisfactory way to distinguish between local and general law. On the other hand, Swift introduced grave discrimination by non-citizens against citizens. The privilege of selecting the court for resolving disputes rested with the non-citizen who could pick the more favorable forum. The resulting far-reaching discrimination

was due to the broad province accorded "general law" in which many matters of seemingly local concern were included. Furthermore, local citizens could move out of the state and bring suit in a federal court if they were disposed to do so; corporations, similarly, could simply reincorporate in another state. More than statutory relief is involved here; the unconstitutionality of Swift is clear. (3) Except in matters governed by the Federal Constitution or by acts of Congress, the law to be applied in any case is the law of the state. There is no federal common law. The federal courts have no power derived from the Constitution or by Congress to declare substantive rules of common law applicable in a state whether they be "local" or "general" in nature. (4) The federal district court was bound to follow the Pennsylvania case law which would have denied recovery to Tompkins (P).

DISSENT: (Butler, J.) Since no constitutional question was presented or argued in the lower court, and a 1937 statute that required notice to the Attorney General whenever a constitutionality of an Act of Congress was raised was not followed, the court's conduct was improper.

EDITOR'S ANALYSIS: Erie can fairly be characterized as the most significant and sweeping decision on civil procedure ever handed down by the U.S. Supreme Court. As interpreted in subsequent decisions, Erie held that while federal courts may apply their own rules of procedure, issues of substantive law must be decided in accord with the applicable state law — usually the state in which the federal court sits. Note, however, how later Supreme Court decisions have made inroads into the broad doctrine enunciated here.

[For more information on Erie, see Casenote Law Outline on Conflict of Laws, Chapter 4, § I, The Erie Doctrine.]

NOTES:

KLAXON v. STENTOR ELECTRIC MFG. CO.
313 U.S. 487 (1941).

NATURE OF CASE: Damages for breach of contract.

FACT SUMMARY: Stentor (P) received judgment for breach of contract based on Klaxon's (D) failure to manufacture and sell certain goods. Klaxon (D) appeals that part of the order allowing interest on the damages from when the suit was filed.

CONCISE RULE OF LAW: Federal district courts must apply the conflict of law rules of the states in which they sit when deciding a case based upon diversity jurisdiction.

FACTS: In 1918, Stentor Electric (P) transferred its entire business to Klaxon (D) in return for a contractual promise by Klaxon (D) to use best efforts to promote the sale of certain items upon which Stentor (P) retained patent rights. Stentor (P) was a New York corporation, Klaxon (D) a Delaware corporation, and the agreement was executed and partially performed in New York. In 1929, Stentor (P), suing in diversity jurisdiction, sued Klaxon (D) in federal district court in Delaware for breach of the agreement. A judgment of $100,000 was rendered in Stentor's (P) favor. Stentor then moved to modify the judgment to add interest at the rate of 6% from the date the action was commenced. The motion was based on a New York statute and was granted by the district court on the grounds that the issue was substantive and that New York law governed the dispute. Klaxon (D) appealed the motion, asserting that the district court was bound to follow the substantive law of Delaware in diversity actions. The Circuit Court of Appeals affirmed on the basis that the New York rule was the "better view."

ISSUE: In a diversity jurisdiction case, must the federal courts apply the conflict of law rules prevailing in the states in which the court sits?

HOLDING AND DECISION: (Reed, J.) Yes. Federal courts cannot make independent determinations of what the law in the state in which they sit should be, but must apply the conflicts rules of the states when deciding diversity jurisdiction cases. There is no independent general law of conflicts. Each state in the federal system is free to determine whether a given matter is to be governed by the law of the forum or some other law. Therefore, there must be uniformity within each state so as to avoid forum shopping between federal and state courts within each state. The proper function of the federal courts is to determine what the state law is, and not what the law should be. Any other decision would lead to a disruption of the equal administration of justice in state and federal courts which sit in the same state and apply the same state law.

EDITOR'S ANALYSIS: The Klaxon case amplifies the Erie rule to include the state conflict of law rules where they apply to outcome determinative issues. On remand, the Circuit Court found that the Delaware conflicts rules referred the issue to N.Y. law, and thus the decision remained the same through the use of differing rules.

[For more information on Erie and state conflict rules, see Casenote Law Outline on Conflict of Laws, Chapter 4, § II, The Klaxon Corollary.]

NOTES:

VAN DUSEN v. BARRACK
376 U.S. 612 (1964).

NATURE OF CASE: Review of order transferring venue in a diversity personal injury action.

FACT SUMMARY: Van Dusen (P) contended that his diversity action should not be transferred on forum non conveniens grounds because the substantive law of the transferee district would be prejudicial.

CONCISE RULE OF LAW: When a diversity case is transferred on forum non conveniens grounds, the substantive law to be applied remains the same.

FACTS: An airline disaster occurring in Massachusetts resulted in over 150 lawsuits, including that of Van Dusen (P), which was filed in Pennsylvania in U.S. district court, jurisdiction being based on diversity. A motion to change venue to Massachusetts was made under 28 U.S.C. § 1404(a), the federal forum non conveniens statute. The motion was granted. Van Dusen (P) appealed, contending that the change of venue would result in a prejudicial change of substantive law. The court of appeals affirmed, and the Supreme Court granted review.

ISSUE: When a diversity case is transferred on forum non conveniens grounds, does the substantive law to be applied remain the same?

HOLDING AND DECISION: (Goldberg, J.) Yes. When a diversity case is transferred on forum non conveniens grounds, the substantive law to be applied remains the same. Nothing in the language or legislative history of § 1404(a) indicates that Congress intended that a transfer thereunder would involve a change of substantive law. Indeed, if such an interpretation were to be given to the section, it could be used as a forum-shopping device, a use which is clearly inconsistent with both congressional and judicial policy. Further, under the Erie doctrine, results in federal courts sitting in diversity should be the same as those in state courts. To hold § 1404(a) to allow a change of substantive law would undercut the policy of Erie. For these reasons, Van Dusen's (P) concerns about a prejudicial change of venue were misplaced. Affirmed.

EDITOR'S ANALYSIS: The present opinion does not determine which law will be applied. It merely states that the transferor court's choice of law rules will be applied. Here, for instance, it was quite possible that Pennsylvania courts would choose to apply Massachusetts law, the very result Van Dusen (P) wanted to avoid.

[For more information on venue transfer in federal courts, see Casenote Law Outline on Conflict of Laws, Chapter 4, § II, The Klaxon Corollary.]

FERENS v. JOHN DEERE CO.
494 U.S. 516 (1989).

NATURE OF CASE: Review of order dismissing a tort action on the ground that the statute of limitations had run.

FACT SUMMARY: To take advantage of Mississippi's six-year statute of limitations for tort actions, Ferens (P) sued Deere (D) there for negligence and products lability and then on grounds of convenience moved to transfer the action to federal court in Pennsylvania, Ferens' (P) state of residence, which had only a two-year statute of limitations.

CONCISE RULE OF LAW: When a party initiates the transfer of an action under 28 U.S.C. § 1404(a), the transferee court must follow the choice-of-law rules applied by the transferor court.

FACTS: Ferens (P), a resident of Pennsylvania, lost his hand when it became caught in his Deere (D) manufactured combine harvester while working with the machine on his Pennsylvania farm. In the third year after the accident, Ferens (P) sued Deere (D), a Delaware corporation with its principal place of business in Illinois, in diversity in Pennsylvania, raising contract and warranty claims. However, Pennsylvania's two-year statute of limitations for tort actions had already expired. In the same year, Ferens (P) filed a second diversity suit against Deere (D), a corporate resident of Mississippi, in federal court in Mississippi, alleging negligence and products liability. Mississippi had a six-year statute of limitations for tort actions. Ferens (P) knew that the federal court, in the exercise of diversity jurisdiction, would follow the Mississippi choice-of-law rules and apply Pennsylvania substantive law to the personal injury claim but would apply Mississippi procedural law to the limitation period. Next, on the assumption that Mississippi choice-of-law rules would still apply, Ferens (P) moved to transfer the second action to the federal court in Pennsylvania on the ground that it was a more convenient forum. Deere (D) did not oppose, and the motion was granted. The district court in Pennsylvania consolidated the transferred tort action with Ferens' (P) warranty action but declined to follow Mississippi's six-year statute of limitations because Ferens (P) as a plaintiff had moved for the transfer. It then dismissed the tort action. The court of appeals affirmed on an appeal by Ferens (P), and the Supreme Court granted review.

ISSUE: When a party initiates the transfer of an action under 28 U.S.C. § 1404(a), must the transferee court follow the choice-of-law rules applied by the transferor court?

HOLDING AND DECISION: (Kennedy, J.) Yes. When a party initiates the transfer of an action under 28 U.S.C. § 1404(a), the transferee court must follow the choice-of-law rules applied by the transferor court. Section 1404(a) states only that a district court may transfer venue for the convenience of the parties and witnesses when in the interest of justice. It says nothing about choice of law and nothing about affording plaintiffs different treatment from defendants. Three independent reasons exist for requiring a transferee court to apply the choice-of-law rules that prevailed in the transferor court when a defendant moved for transfer, namely, § 1404(a) should not deprive parties of state law advantages that exist absent diversity jurisdiction; it should not create or multiply opportunities for forum shopping; and the decision to transfer should turn on considerations of convenience and the interest of justice rather than on possible prejudice resulting from a change of law. First, applying the transferor court law when a plaintiff requests a transfer will not deprive the plaintiff of any state law advantages. A defendant also will not lose legal advantage since the same law would have applied if the motion had not been made. Applying the transferee law, by contrast, would undermine the Erie rule in that initiating a transfer would change the state law applicable to a diversity suit. Second, even without § 1404(a), a plaintiff already has the option of shopping for a forum with the most favorable law. Finally, if the law were to change following a transfer requested by a plaintiff, a district court would be reluctant to grant a transfer that would prejudice the defendant, and the plaintiff would not request such a transfer even if it were more convenient if the law to be applied was unfavorable. Thus, the desire to take a punitive view of the Ferens' (P) actions should not obscure the systematic costs of litigating in an inconvenient forum. Reversed and remanded.

DISSENT: (Scalia, J.) This case involves an interpretation of the Rules of Decision Act, which requires a federal court to apply, in diversity cases, the law of the state in which it sits. In filing a diversity action in the federal court in Mississippi and then moving to transfer the case to the federal court in Pennsylvania, Ferens (P) was seeking the use of a Pennsylvania federal court instead of a Pennsylvania state court in order to obtain application of a different substantive law, namely, the Mississippi choice-of-law rules, which would require application of that state's six-year statute of limitations. Thus, requiring transferee courts to apply the choice-of-law rules that apply in the transferor court when a plaintiff moves for the transfer violates the Act and encourages forum shopping by allowing the plaintiff to appropriate the law of forum in which he does not intend to litigate.

EDITOR'S ANALYSIS: Justice Kennedy attempted to preempt Justice Scalia's argument that the decision would result in forum shopping between federal and state courts by pointing out that, if it does make selection of the most favorable law more convenient, it does no more than recognize a choice that already existed; Ferens (P) could have sued in Mississippi state court. However, that argument assumes that litigating in an inconvenient forum would not be cost prohibitive. Since cost is a deciding factor in most litigation, the decision has the added effect of encouraging more litigation, not foreclosing it, which, coincidentally, statutes of limitation are supposed to do.

[For more information on federal court transfers, see Casenote Law Outline on Conflict of Laws, Chapter 2, § IV, Grounds for not Exercising Jurisdiction.]

STEWART ORGANIZATION, INC. v. RICOH CORP
108 S. Ct. 2239 (1988).

NATURE OF CASE: Review of order reversing denial of motion to transfer venue.

FACT SUMMARY: A district court, entertaining a motion to transfer venue in a diversity case, felt obligated to apply state law which disfavored contractual forum selection clauses and consequently denied the motion.

CONCISE RULE OF LAW: In a motion to transfer venue, a federal court sitting in diversity should apply federal law regarding contractual forum-selection clauses.

FACTS: Stewart Organization, Inc. (P) filed an action in U.S. District Court in Alabama, alleging breach of a dealership agreement it had entered with Ricoh Corp. (D). Ricoh (D) moved to transfer venue to the Southern District of New York, pursuant to a contractual forum-selection clause. The district court, sitting in diversity, felt constrained to apply Alabama state law, which looked unfavorably upon forum-selection clauses, and denied the motion. The Court of Appeals for the Eleventh Circuit, en banc, reversed, holding venue to be a matter of federal procedure. The Supreme Court granted review.

ISSUE: In a motion to transfer venue, should a federal court sitting in diversity apply federal law regarding contractual forum-selection clauses?

HOLDING AND DECISION: (Marshall, J.) Yes. In a motion to transfer venue, a federal court sitting in diversity should apply federal law regarding contractual forum-selection clauses. Even in a diversity case, when a federal law controls a point at issue, that law will take precedence over any otherwise applicable state law. Here, 28 U.S.C. § 1404(a) governs venue transfer. The section is intended to place discretion in district court's ruling on such motions according to an individualized, case-by-case analysis of convenience and fairness. Clearly, a forum-selection clause is one such factor a district court should consider. Consequently, forum-selection matters are to by analyzed with reference to federal law, not state law. Here, federal law requires that a forum-selection clause be one of possibly many factors to be determined; Alabama law would appear to give it determinative weight. For these reasons, the matter must be remanded for a determination in light of § 1404(a). Affirmed.

DISSENT: (Scalia, J.) The issue of forum-selection clauses does not fall within § 1404(a). This being so, state law should be applied, per the Erie doctrine.

CONCURRENCE: (Kennedy, J.) The federal judiciary should clearly encourage the enforcement of forum-selection clauses.

EDITOR'S ANALYSIS: This case should not be seen as holding forum selection clauses sacrosanct. It is clear that such clauses are merely one factor to be considered by a court ruling on a § 1404(a) motion. The concurrence would appear to want to make such clauses more determinative than does the main opinion.

[For more information on forum-selection clauses, see Casenote Law Outline on Conflict of Laws, Chapter 2, § IV, Grounds for not Exercising Jurisdiction.]

NOTES:

IN RE AIR CRASH DISASTER NEAR NEW ORLEANS
821 F.2d 1147 (5th Cir. 1987).

NATURE OF CASE: Appeal of denial of motion to dismiss on the basis of forum non conveniens in an action to recover for injuries.

FACT SUMMARY: Uruguay citizens (P) sued Pan American (D) for injuries suffered in an airline crash.

CONCISE RULE OF LAW: In applying forum non-conveniens in a diversity action, a federal court applies federal forum non-conveniens law.

FACTS: Foreign citizens (P) sued Pan American (D) in a Louisiana federal court for injuries suffered as a result of an airline crash near New Orleans. Pan American (D) invoked the doctrine of forum non-conveniens in a motion to dismiss, arguing that the Plaintiffs' home country of Uruguay was the proper forum for their claims. The district court denied the Defendant's motion. The Fifth Circuit took the case en banc.

ISSUE: In applying forum non-conveniens in a diversity action, does a federal court apply the forum non-conveniens law of the state in which it sits rather than federal forum non-conveniens law? Does applying federal forum non-conveniens hinder the "twin aims" of *ERIE*?

HOLDING AND DECISION: (Hill, J.) No. A federal court sitting in a diversity action is required to apply the federal law of forum non-conveniens when addressing a motion to dismiss a plaintiff's case for forum non-conveniens. Under *ERIE*, applying federal forum non-conveniens law advances, rather than hinders, the twin aims of *ERIE*. The interests of the federal forum in self-regulation, in administrative independence, and in self-management are more important than the disruption of uniformity created by applying federal forum non-convenience in diversity cases. Although the *ERIE* concern of forum shopping would be present if federal law were used, the other interests of the federal courts tilt the scales in favor of applying federal law. The interests of federal courts in maintaining the federal docket, even in diversity cases, are powerful. Such interests are the ability to control the litigation and to prevent process from becoming an instrument of abuse, injustice, and oppression. Federal forum interests in self-management therefore point forcefully toward applying federal law under the second aim of *ERIE*. The analysis of *ERIE*'s twin aims in the context of selecting federal or state forum selection law produces conflicting indications on how to resolve the issue. The aim of dissuading forum shopping points to applying Louisiana law. The other aim, however, points to applying federal law as a matter of internal consistency and administration, and therefore federal law will be applied. Reversed.

CONCURRENCE: (Higginbotham, J.) The majority's interpretations of the twin aims of *ERIE* place too little emphasis on the state law interests. It likewise places too much emphasis on federal forum interests in self-administration. The twin aims of *ERIE* are not competing aims. With forum non-conveniens we're deferring to a judge-made rule, not to Congress. We're rejecting a decision by Louisiana not to recognize forum non-conveniens. Louisiana citizens will be discriminated against.

EDITOR'S ANALYSIS: The federal court in this case chose to hold onto its self-regulation powers. In most states, the state and federal forum non-conveniens laws are identical. In Louisiana, however, state forum non-conveniens law is substantially different from federal forum non-conveniens law, as Louisiana doesn't permit a forum non-conveniens dismissal to a foreign forum.

SEMTEK INT'L INC. v. LOCKHEED MARTIN CORP.
California company (P) v. Maryland company (D)
531 U.S. 497 (2001).

NATURE OF CASE: Review of dismissal of a state breach of contract action due to the res judicata effect of a federal diversity judgment.

FACT SUMMARY: After a federal district court dismissed a breach of contract complaint under California's two-year statute of limitations, Semtek (P) filed the same action in Maryland, which has a longer statute of limitations, but the court dismissed the case on res judicata grounds.

CONCISE RULE OF LAW: Where there is no conflict with federal interests, the claim preclusive effect of a dismissal by a federal court sitting in diversity should be determined according to the law of the state in which the federal court is sitting.

FACTS: Semtek (P) sued Lockheed (D) for breach of contract in California state court and Lockheed (D) removed the case to federal court. After the court dismissed the action with prejudice because the statute of limitations had run, Semtek (P) filed the same complaint in Maryland, where Lockheed was a citizen and the statute of limitations was longer. The Maryland trial court granted Lockheed's (D) motion to dismiss for res judicata and Semtek (P) appealed, arguing that a California state court would not have accorded claim preclusive effect to a statute of limitations dismissal by one of its own courts. The Maryland appeals court affirmed the dismissal, holding that the res judicata effect of a federal diversity judgment was a matter of federal law and that the judgment was preclusive. The Supreme Court granted certiorari.

ISSUE: Where there is no conflict with federal interests, should the claim preclusive effect of a dismissal by a federal court sitting in diversity be determined according to the law of the state in which the federal court is sitting?

HOLDING AND DECISION: (Scalia, J.) Yes. Where there is no conflict with federal interests, the claim preclusive effect of a dismissal by a federal court sitting in diversity should be determined according to the law of the state in which the federal court is sitting. The claim preclusive effect, in Maryland, of the California diversity judgment should not be based on either the precedent in Dupasseur v. Rochereau, a case decided under the Conformity Act of 1872, which required federal courts to apply the procedural law of the forum state, or on FRCP 14(b). Despite the repeal of the Conformity Act and the promulgation of the Erie doctrine, the result decreed by Dupasseur continues to be correct for diversity cases. Since state law is at issue, there is no need for a uniform federal rule. The law that should be applied is that law that would be applied by state courts in the state in which the federal diversity court sits. Reversed and remanded.

EDITOR'S ANALYSIS: Since California would not have accorded claim preclusive effect, it was error for the Maryland court to do so. Under Erie, federal courts are to apply the substantive state law of the state in which they sit. When the application of state law would influence the outcome of the case, state law should be applied.

QUICKNOTES

CERTIORARI - A discretionary writ issued by a superior court to an inferior court in order to review the lower court's decisions; the Supreme Court's writ ordering such review.

ERIE DOCTRINE - Federal courts must apply state substantive law and federal procedural law.

DIVERSITY JURISDICTION - The authority of a federal court to hear and determine cases involving $75,000 or more and in which the parties are citizens of different states, or in which one party is an alien.

RES JUDICATA - The rule of law that a final judgment by a court precludes subsequent litigation between the parties regarding the same cause of action.

CLEARFIELD TRUST CO. v. UNITED STATES
318 U.S. 363 (1943).

NATURE OF CASE: Review of reversal of dismissal of action for reimbursement of payment on commercial paper.

FACT SUMMARY: In an action by the Government (P) to recover on a draft drawn on it that contained a forged endorsement, the Government (P) argued that federal law applied.

CONCISE RULE OF LAW: In an action based on commercial paper issued by the U.S. government, federal law controls.

FACTS: The U.S. Treasury issued a draft, drawn on a Federal Reserve Bank, payable to one Barner for work performed for the WPA. The check was intercepted by a unknown individual, who presented it with a forged endorsement to J.C. Penney Co. (D), which cashed it. The check was in turn negotiated to Clearfield Trust Co. (D), which in turn negotiated it to the Federal Reserve Bank, with the endorsement "prior endorsements guaranteed." Barner eventually requested and was given payment. The Government (P) brought an action in U.S. district court in Philadelphia, seeking reimbursement. The district court, applying Pennsylvania law, held the Government (P) to have unreasonably delayed in giving notice of the forgery to Clearfield (D) and dismissed. The court of appeals reversed, holding federal law applicable. The Supreme Court granted review.

ISSUE: Does federal law control in an action based on commercial paper issued by the U.S. government?

HOLDING AND DECISION: (Douglas, J.) Yes. In an action based on commercial paper issued by the U.S. government, federal law applies. When the federal government issues funds to pay its debts, it is exercising a power that emanates from the U.S. Constitution, not state law. Beyond this, the issuance commercial paper by the U.S. government is on a vast scale, and to hold the patchwork of state laws and regulations controlling would subject suits on such paper to great uncertainty. The necessity for a uniform rule is clear, and consequently federal law must control. [The Court went on to hold that the delay by the Government (P) in notifying Clearfield (D) of the forgery was not prejudicial, and that therefore the suit should be allowed to proceed.] Affirmed.

EDITOR'S ANALYSIS: The present case is an example of federal common law. Erie R.R. v. Tompkins, 304 U.S. 64 (1938), abolished federal general common law, but not federal common law. Federal common law is that decisional law which relates to rights or obligations having origins in federal constitutional or statutory law.

[For more information on federal common law, see Casenote Law Outline on Conflict of Laws, Chapter 4, § IV, Federal Common Law.]

NOTES:

ILLINOIS v. CITY OF MILWAUKEE
406 U.S. 91 (1972).

NATURE OF CASE: Motion for leave to file a nuisance action in the Supreme Court.

FACT SUMMARY: Illinois (P) urged the Supreme Court to exercise its original jurisdiction in a nuisance action between it and several municipal entities.

CONCISE RULE OF LAW: The Supreme Court should not exercise its original jurisdiction in an action by a state against alleged polluters.

FACTS: Illinois (P), complaining of the discharge of raw sewage into Lake Michigan by the city of Milwaukee, (D), sought leave to file an action against it and other municipal entities, asking it to invoke its original jurisdiction under Article III of the Constitution.

ISSUE: Should the Supreme Court exercise its original jurisdiction in an action by a state against alleged polluters?

HOLDING AND DECISION: (Douglas, J.) No. The Supreme Court should not exercise its original jurisdiction in an action by a state against alleged polluters. The Constitution provides that this Court shall have original jurisdiction in all cases where a state is a party. However, this provision has been interpreted to be discretionary; this Court may assume original jurisdiction, but need not. Whether it shall do so in any given case depends to a large extent upon the availability of an alternate forum. Under 28 U.S.C. § 1331(a), U.S. district courts have jurisdiction over actions involving the laws, Constitution, or treaties of the United States. Here, there is no specific federal statute dealing with the discharge of raw sewage into public waters. However, the federal Water Pollution Control Act makes it clear that dealing with water pollution is a policy issue into which the federal government has inserted itself. There are and no doubt will be numerous court decisions dealing with the discharge of pollutants into waters. This Court is of the view that "laws," as provided by § 1331(a), refers not only to statutes, but to federal common law as well. Since the issue Illinois (P) wishes to litigate relates to federal law, federal district court is an available forum. Since an alternative forum is available, this Court should decline Illinois' (P) invitation to assume original jurisdiction. Motion denied.

EDITOR'S ANALYSIS: The jurisdiction of the Supreme Court is defined at Article III, § 2, clause 2, of the Constitution. This section is silent as to original jurisdiction being mandatory or discretionary. Under the Constitution, Congress has the power to determine the jurisdiction of the federal courts. Exercising this authority, Congress enacted 28 U.S.C. § 125, which clarified the situation by making original jurisdiction mandatory only in suits between states.

[For more information on federal common law, see Casenote Law Outline on Conflict of Laws, Chapter 4, § IV, Federal Common Law.]

NOTES:

DURFEE v. DUKE
375 U.S. 106 (1963).

NATURE OF CASE: Appeal from an action to determine ownership to land.

FACT SUMMARY: After Durfee (D) won a Nebraska case adjudicating the location of certain land to be in Nebraska and to be his, Duke (P) began a new action in Missouri, where the U. S. Court of Appeals held the Nebraska action not to be res judicata on the issues.

CONCISE RULE OF LAW: A judgment is entitled to full faith and credit, even as to questions of jurisdiction, when the second court's inquiry discloses that those questions have been fully and fairly litigated and finally decided in the court which rendered the original judgment.

FACTS: Durfee (D) brought an action in Nebraska to quiet title to certain bottom land along the Missouri River. The river's main channel is the boundary between Nebraska and Missouri. Nebraska had jurisdiction over the subject matter only if the land was, in fact, in Nebraska. In full litigation of the issues, the Nebraska court found that it had jurisdiction. It then determined that Durfee (D) owned the land. The Nebraska Supreme Court affirmed and Duke (P) did not appeal further. Two months later, Duke (P) brought suit in Missouri to quiet title to the same land. By diversity of citizenship, the action was removed to federal district court, which decided that while the land appeared to be in Missouri, the Nebraska ruling was res judicata on the issues and binding. The court of appeals reversed, and Durfee (D) appealed.

ISSUE: Is a judgment entitled to full faith and credit, even as to questions of jurisdiction, when the second court's inquiry discloses that those questions have been fully and fairly litigated and finally decided in the court which rendered the original judgment?

HOLDING AND DECISION: (Stewart, J.) Yes. A judgment is entitled to full faith and credit, even as to questions of jurisdiction, when the second court's inquiry discloses that those questions have been fully and fairly litigated and finally decided in the court which rendered the original judgment. Public policy requires that litigation come to an end at some time. The litigants must reach a point where they will be bound by the ruling. The general rule is no different when the issue is one of jurisdiction. When a case is fully heard and there has been no fraud, the parties are bound by the court to which they submitted their dispute. While certain exceptions such as federal preemption or sovereign immunity exist, none apply here. All issues were fully litigated in the Nebraska courts including the issue of jurisdiction. Full faith and credit must be given the Nebraska ruling. Reversed.

EDITOR'S ANALYSIS: The older view allowed a second court to examine the jurisdictional basis upon which the first court ruled.

Jurisdiction is no longer a "magic word," but is approached as any other issue. Restatement of Conflicts, Second, § 97, suggests a balancing test to determine whether subject matter jurisdiction should be allowed to be collaterally attacked. Such balancing depends on policy considerations including whether the determination is based on questions of fact or law, and whether the question was actually litigated.

[For more information on conclusive nature of foreign findings, see Casenote Law Outline on Conflict of Laws, Chapter 9, § IV, Full Faith and Credit and Jurisdictional Issues.]

NOTES:

FALL v. EASTIN
215 U.S. 1 (1909).

NATURE OF CASE: Review of dismissal of action to quiet title and cancel a deed.

FACT SUMMARY: Fall (P) sought to enforce in the Nebraska courts a Washington state judgment giving her title to property in Nebraska.

CONCISE RULE OF LAW: A court need not respect a judgment of another state purporting to affect title to land located in the state where the judgment is sought to be enforced.

FACTS: Fall (P) and her husband were Washington residents. A Washington court, in granting them a divorce, awarded Fall (P) certain land situated in Nebraska that she and her husband had jointly owned. While the action was pending, the husband executed a deed to the property in favor of a relative, who subsequently deeded it to Eastin (D). Fall (P) brought an action in a Nebraska court, seeking to enforce the decree giving her title. The trial court dismissed, and the Nebraska Supreme Court affirmed. The Supreme Court granted review.

ISSUE: Must a court respect a judgment of another state purporting to affect title to land located in the state where the judgment is sought to be enforced?

HOLDING AND DECISION: (McKenna, J.) No. A court need not respect a judgment of another state purporting to affect title to land located in the state where the judgment is sought to be enforced. With respect to a judgment in rem, when a court does not have jurisdiction over the res in issue, it cannot affect it by decree. Since a decree of this nature has no validity, it need not be respected by another state under the Full Faith and Credit Clause. It is true that a court in equity can compel a party to convey property when it acts in personam, and such a decree must be respected. However, the decree sought to be enforced here was not such a decree. The decree was of the in rem variety and cannot be enforced. Affirmed.

CONCURRENCE: (Holmes, J.) If Eastin (D) were not an innocent purchaser, the decree could be enforced.

EDITOR'S ANALYSIS: There is little doubt that had Fall (P) been proceeding against her ex-husband rather than an assignee, she would have been successful. The Washington court, having jurisdiction over the ex-husband, could have entered an injunction compelling transfer. Such a judgment would have been enforceable in other states.

[For more information on foreign land decrees, see Casenote Law Outline on Conflict of Laws, Chapter 9, § V, Foreign Land Decrees.]

NOTES:

KALB v. FEUERSTEIN
308 U.S. 433 (1940).

NATURE OF CASE: Review of dismissal of actions for damages and to cancel a sheriff's sale.

FACT SUMMARY: Kalb (P), who had lost property due to foreclosure during the pendency of a bankruptcy proceeding, collaterally attacked the sale.

CONCISE RULE OF LAW: A foreclosure sale effected during the pendency of the mortgagor's bankruptcy may be collaterally attacked.

FACTS: Kalb (P) owned a farm, which he had mortgaged. After subsequently falling into arrears in payment, he petitioned for bankruptcy. Despite the bankruptcy, a sheriff's sale was held, and the property was sold. Kalb (P) field an action seeking to set aside the sale and a companion action seeking damages. The trial court dismissed the actions, and the Wisconsin Supreme Court affirmed. The Supreme Court granted review.

ISSUE: May a foreclosure sale effected during the pendency of the mortgagor's bankruptcy be collaterally attacked?

HOLDING AND DECISION: (Black, J.) Yes. A foreclosure sale effected during the pendency of the Mortgagor's bankruptcy may be collaterally attacked. It is generally true that a judgment by a court of competent jurisdiction bears a presumption of regularity and may not be subjected to collateral attack. However, when Congress, exercising its constitutional authority, preempts the area and prohibits state court action, any such action is void and may be collaterally attacked. Here, the bankruptcy petition automatically stayed any state court action on property belonging to Kalb (P). The foreclosure sale was therefore void and subject to collateral attack.

EDITOR'S ANALYSIS: Collateral attacks are not usually made in the state where the underlying judgment being attacked was issued. The classic situation of this sort is where a default judgment is rendered, which is then collaterally attacked on jurisdictional grounds in an enforcement proceeding. A court judgment where jurisdiction was absent is void and not entitled to full faith and credit.

[For more information on jurisdiction, see Casenote Law Outline on Conflict of Laws, Chapter 9, § IV, Full Faith and Credit and Jurisdictional Issues.]

NOTES:

FAUNTLEROY v. LUM
210 U.S. 230 (1908).

NATURE OF CASE: Suit to enforce contract indebtedness.

FACT SUMMARY: Lum (P) brought suit in Mississippi to enforce a Missouri judgment in his favor arising out of a contract executed and performed in Mississippi but not enforceable there due to illegality.

CONCISE RULE OF LAW: A judgment rendered by a court of competent jurisdiction in one state is entitled to full faith and credit in another state notwithstanding any errors of law in the judgment or the fact that the underlying cause of action is prohibited in the second state.

FACTS: Lum's (P) predecessor in interest entered into a commodities futures contract with Fauntleroy (D) in Mississippi. Such contracts were in violation of both civil and criminal statutes of Mississippi. An arbitration proceeding resulted in an award to Lum (P) under the contract. Lum (P) then sued in Missouri to enforce the award and judgment was granted in his favor. He then brought suit in Mississippi to enforce the Missouri judgment but the Mississippi court refused enforcement because to do so would be in violation of express public policy.

ISSUE: Must the courts of one state give full faith and credit enforcement to the judgment of another state based on an agreement that violates the public policy of the state asked to enforce the judgment?

HOLDING AND DECISION: (Holmes, J.) Yes. The judgment of a state court should have the same credit, validity, and effect in every other court in the United States that it had in the state where it was pronounced, and whatever pleas would be good to a suit thereon in such state, and no others, could be pleaded in any other court of the United States. It the judgment of the Missouri court was based on a mistake of Mississippi law, then that judgment could have been appealed in Missouri. Since it was not, it is as enforceable in Mississippi as it would be in Missouri.

DISSENT: (White, J.) No state is under the obligation to give effect to judgments which are, in the enforcing state, illegal and prohibited.

EDITOR'S ANALYSIS: The merits of a foreign judgment can never be examined when enforcement is sought in the forum state. The only legitimate challenge can be to the jurisdiction, personal or subject matter, of the foreign court to render the judgment. The majority opinion in this case has been affirmed as late as 1949 by the Supreme Court.

[For more information on judgments based on errors of law, see Casenote Law Outline on Conflict of Laws, Chapter 9, § II, Conclusiveness of Judgments.]

NOTES:

THOMAS v. WASHINGTON GAS LIGHT CO.
448 U.S. 261 (1980).

NATURE OF CASE: Action seeking disability benefits.

FACT SUMMARY: Having already sought and obtained disability benefits under applicable Virginia law, Thomas (P) sought a supplemental award under the District of Columbia's compensation act.

CONCISE RULE OF LAW: A state has no legitimate interest in preventing another state from granting a supplemental compensation award when that second state would have had the power to apply its worker's compensation law in the first instance.

FACTS: Thomas (P), a District of Columbia resident hired there by Washington Gas (D), was injured while at work in Virginia. Initially, he sought and recovered benefits pursuant to an award by the Virginia Industrial Commission. He later brought an action in the District of Columbia seeking additional compensation under its Worker's Compensation Act. Washington (D) argued that the District's obligation to give the prior award full faith and credit precluded a second, supplemental award in the District. The administrative law judge held that the Virginia award did not, by its terms, preclude a further award of compensation and awarded supplemental benefits. The Benefits Review Board upheld the award, but the U.S. Court of Appeals reversed on Full Faith and Credit grounds.

ISSUE: Does a state which has awarded compensation have a legitimate interest in preventing a second state that would have had the power to apply its compensation law in the first place from granting a supplemental compensation award?

HOLDING AND DECISION: (Stevens, J.) No. A state which has awarded compensation does not have any legitimate interest in preventing a second state from granting a supplemental compensation award when that second state would have had the power to apply its workmen's compensation law in the first place. The critical difference between a court of general jurisdiction and an administrative agency with limited statutory authority forecloses the conclusion that constitutional rules applicable to court judgments are necessarily applicable to worker's compensation awards. The Virginia Commission could and did establish the full measure of Thomas' (P) rights under the law of Virginia. Since it had no authority and was not requested to pass on his rights under District of Columbia law, there can be no constitutional objection to a fresh adjudication of those rights. The Full Faith and Credit Clause should not be construed to preclude successive worker's compensation awards. Reversed.

CONCURRENCE: (White, J.) I agree that the judgment of the court of appeals should be reversed, but cannot join in the reasoning by which the plurality reaches that result. Although I find the McCartin decision to rest on questionable foundations, I am not prepared to join in overruling it. That decision, which is limited to the worker's compensation area, provides that the compensation act of the first state must contain "unmistakable" language directed at precluding a supplemental compensation award in another state before a supplemental award by another state can be precluded. There is no such language in the Virginia Compensation Act. Thus, the supplemental award by the District was proper.

DISSENT: (Rehnquist, J.) The plurality gives insufficient weight to the interest of Virginia in fashioning its weighing of the interests tests

EDITOR'S ANALYSIS: Critics of this decision suggest that the Court was looking for a way to protect workers who are often coerced or maneuvered into filing their claims in jurisdictions amenable to their employers. However, any time there is fraud, imposition, or mistake in the filing of a claim, the ultimate award could be vacated upon filing of a timely motion. That would leave the claimant free to pursue his remedy in another more amenable jurisdiction.

[For more information on full faith and credit and worker's compensation cases, see Casenote Law Outline on Conflict of Laws, Chapter 9, § II, Conclusiveness of Judgments.]

NOTES:

BAKER v. GENERAL MOTORS CORP.
522 U.S. 222 (1998).

NATURE OF CASE: Review of reversal of judgment enforcing an injunction forbidding a witness from appearing in certain court proceedings.

FACT SUMMARY: After an injunction had been issued in one state court prohibiting a former employee from testifying as a witness, Baker (P) subpoenaed the same former employee to appear as a witness in another state in litigation against the same employer, GM (D).

CONCISE RULE OF LAW: Orders commanding action or inaction may be denied enforcement in a sister state when they purport to accomplish an official act within the exclusive province of that other state or interfere with litigation over which the ordering state has no authority.

FACTS: In settlement of claims arising from the discharge of Elwell, a former employee of GM (D), a state court in Michigan issued a permanent injunction barring Elwell from testifying, without the prior written consent of GM (D), as a witness of any kind in any litigation involving GM (D). GM (D) separately agreed, however, that if Elwell were ordered to testify by a court, such testimony would not be actionable. The Bakers (P) sued GM (D) in Missouri and subpoenaed Elwell to appear as a witness in their suit. The federal district court in Missouri allowed the Bakers (P) to depose Elwell and call him as a witness at trial. Relying on the Full Faith and Credit Clause, the Eighth Circuit reversed, ruling that the testimony should not have been admitted. The Supreme Court granted review.

ISSUE: May orders commanding action or inaction be denied enforcement in a sister state when they purport to accomplish an official act within the exclusive province of that other state or interfere with litigation over which the ordering state has no authority?

HOLDING AND DECISION: (Ginsberg, J.) Yes. Orders commanding action or inaction may be denied enforcement in a sister state when they purport to accomplish an official act within the exclusive province of that other state or interfere with litigation over which the ordering state has no authority. In this case, the Michigan decree ordering the injunction cannot determine evidentiary issues in a lawsuit brought by parties who were not subject to the jurisdiction of the Michigan court. The Full Faith and Credit Clause mandates recognition only of dispositions that Michigan has the authority to order. A Michigan decree cannot command obedience elsewhere on a matter the Michigan court lacks authority to resolve. Reversed.

CONCURRENCE: (Scalia, J.) It has been established that the judgment of a state court cannot be enforced out of the state by an execution issued within it.

CONCURRENCE: (Kennedy, J.) The case is controlled by well-settled full faith and credit principles which render the majority's extended analysis unnecessary. Courts need give a prior judgment no more force or effect than the issuing state gives it. Since the Bakers (P) were not parties to the Michigan proceedings and had no opportunity to litigate any of the issues presented, it appears that Michigan law would not treat them as bound by the judgment.

EDITOR'S ANALYSIS: The Court relied on precedent in reaching its decision. Earlier cases considered the transfer of title to land in another state to be an "official act within the exclusive province" of the situs state. The Court, however, made the point that there is no "roving 'public policy' exception" to judgment recognition under the Full Faith and Credit Clause.

[For more information on gender and citizenship, see Casenote Law Outline on Conflict of Laws, Chapter 9, § I, Recognition and Enforcement Practices.]

NOTES:

UNION NATIONAL BANK v. LAMB
337 U.S. 38 (1949).

NATURE OF CASE: Review of order dismissing action to enforce sister-state judgment.

FACT SUMMARY: Union National (P) sought to enforce a Colorado judgment in Missouri which, though still valid in Colorado, would have lapsed if entered in Missouri.

CONCISE RULE OF LAW: A judgment still vital in the state in which it was rendered should be enforced even if it would have lapsed in the state in which enforcement is sought.

FACTS: Union National Bank (P) obtained a judgment against Lamb (D) in Colorado in 1927. In 1945, it instituted an enforcement action against Lamb (D) in Missouri. Under Missouri law, the judgment was no longer valid due to passage of time. Under Colorado law it was still valid. The Missouri court, citing Missouri's lapse period, dismissed. The Supreme Court granted review.

ISSUE: Will a judgment still vital in the state in which it was rendered be enforced even if it would have lapsed in the state in which enforcement is sought?

HOLDING AND DECISION: (Douglas, J.) Yes. A judgment still vital in the state in which it was rendered should be enforced even if it would have lapsed in the state in which enforcement is sought. When a state has jurisdiction over a suit and renders a valid judgment thereon, under the Full Faith and Credit Clause this judgment cannot be impeached in another state even if it could not have been rendered there. Any other result would defeat the aim of the Full Faith and Credit Clause and the statute enacted under it. Here, the judgment was validly rendered in Colorado, and Missouri's lapse statute cannot defeat its enforceability. Reversed.

EDITOR'S ANALYSIS: The Court had previously visited the issue here in Koche v. McDonald, 275 U.S. 449 (1928). That case involved an Oregon judgment which would have been void if rendered in Washington. The Court mandated that Washington enforce the Oregon judgment. The reasoning was basically the same.

[For more information on full faith and credit procedures, see Casenote Law Outline on Conflict of Laws, Chapter 9, § I, Recognition and Enforcement Practices.]

NOTES:

WATKINS v. CONWAY
385 U.S. 188 (1966).

NATURE OF CASE: Suit to enforce a sister state judgment.

FACT SUMMARY: Watkins (P) obtained a tort judgment against Conway (D) in Florida. Over five years later, he sought enforcement of that judgment in Georgia despite a Georgia statute barring enforcement of foreign judgments over five years old.

CONCISE RULE OF LAW: A state may not impose a discriminatory statute of limitations on foreign judgments to bar their enforcement while permitting enforcement of local judgments of similar age.

FACTS: Watkins (P) sued Conway (D) in Florida and obtained a $25,000 tort judgment in that state. Five years and one day later, Watkins (P) brought suit in Georgia to enforce the Florida judgment. Summary judgment was granted to Conway (D) on the basis of a Georgia statute that barred enforcement of a foreign judgment more than five years after it was rendered. Watkins (P) appealed, contending that the bar was a denial of full faith and credit and equal protection, since Georgia permitted a longer statute of limitations on domestic judgments.

ISSUE: May a state discriminatorily impose a shorter statute of limitations on foreign judgments than it imposes on local judgments?

HOLDING AND DECISION: (Per Curiam) No. If the Georgia statute were applied so as to extend a shorter statute on foreign judgments merely because they were rendered outside the state, it would violate full faith and credit and equal protection. However, the statute, as applied, does not prevent Watkins (P) from reviving his judgment in Florida, since the Georgia statute would then run from the revival date. The only circumstance where the Georgia statute would impose a shorter time limit would be where that limit was imposed by the rendering state. As such, it operates directly in accord with full faith and credit, since it follows the law of the rendering state. Summary judgment affirmed, although Watkins (P) can revive the judgment and sue anew in Georgia.

EDITOR'S ANALYSIS: The effect of the Georgia statute was to prevent enforcement of a sister state judgment that would be barred from enforcement in the sister state. Florida had a twenty-year statute of limitations so that revival would not present a problem. But if Florida had a four-year nonrevivable statute, Georgia would not be obligated to enforce a Florida judgment unenforceable in Florida.

[For more information on statutes of limitations, see Casenote Law Outline on Conflict of Laws, Chapter 5, § II, Classifying Rules as Substantive or Procedural.]

NOTES:

TREINIES v. SUNSHINE MINING CO.
308 U.S. 66 (1939).

NATURE OF CASE: Review of interpleader decree.

FACT SUMMARY: In an interpleader action based on inconsistent court decrees, Treinies (D) attempted to raise a jurisdictional issue that had been addressed in a prior court proceeding.

CONCISE RULE OF LAW: A jurisdictional issue decided in one court proceeding may not be relitigated in an interpleader action.

FACTS: A dispute arose between Treinies (D) and Mason (D) over certain shares of stock in Sunshine Mining Co. (P). Mason (D) obtained an Idaho court judgment giving her a one-half interest in the shares. Treinies (D) appeared in that action and actually litigated it. Part of the Idaho court decree consisted of a finding that Washington lacked jurisdiction over the shares. At this time, Treinies (D) was litigating her own suit in Washington. The Washington court awarded all the shares to Treinies (D). Sunshine Mining Co. (P) filed a federal interpleader action, based on diversity, seeking an adjudication of its obligations. The district court held the Washington decree barred by the prior Idaho decree. The Court of Appeals for the Ninth Circuit affirmed, and the Supreme Court granted review.

ISSUE: May a jurisdictional issue decided in one court proceeding be relitigated in an interpleader action?

HOLDING AND DECISION: (Reed, J.) No. A jurisdictional issue decided in one court proceeding may not be relitigated in an interpleader action. The principles of res judicata under the Full Faith and Credit Clause apply to questions of jurisdiction as well as to substantive issues. Here, the question of the jurisdiction of Idaho to render a judgment was actually litigated by Treinies (D) in the Idaho court action. Therefore, he may not collaterally attack it in the present interpleader action. This being so, the holdings below were correct. Affirmed.

EDITOR'S ANALYSIS: Collateral attack is the principal means of challenging a court's jurisdiction. To do this, a party must default in the initial proceeding. If a party appears and actually litigates the matter, subsequent jurisdictional objections are waived. This is what occurred here.

[For more information on jurisdiction, see Casenote Law Outline on Conflict of Laws, Chapter 9, § IV, Full Faith and Credit and Jurisdictional Issues.]

NOTES:

ESTIN v. ESTIN
334 U.S. 541 (1948).

NATURE OF CASE: Review of award of damages for spousal arrearages.

FACT SUMMARY: Mr. Estin (D), having obtained an ex parte divorce in Nevada, contended that an earlier New York separation order, which included alimony provisions, had been voided.

CONCISE RULE OF LAW: An ex parte divorce in one state will not void a prior support order from another state.

FACTS: Mr. Estin (D) moved out of the parties' household, which was located in New York. Mrs. Estin (P) obtained in New York an order of separation, which included an alimony provision. Mr. Estin (D) later moved to Nevada, and there he obtained an ex parte divorce which included no order of support. Mrs. Estin (P) later brought an action in New York for support arrearages based on the New York decree. The trial court entered a judgment awarding damages. This was affirmed on appeal, and the Supreme Court granted review upon Mr. Estin's (D) argument that the Nevada decree superseded and voided the New York decree.

ISSUE: Will an ex parte divorce in one state void a prior support order from another state?

HOLDING AND DECISION: (Douglas, J.) No. An ex parte divorce in one state will not void a prior support order from another state. A state has a considerable interest in regulating the marital status of its domiciliaries as such status affects the legitimacy of offspring and can be the basis for matters of criminal and debtor/creditor law. Therefore, the state should have the power to guard its interests by allowing its domiciliaries to proceed ex parte in marital proceedings, and the Full Faith and Credit Clause demands that other states respect such orders. However, a state may not, in an ex parte divorce proceeding, affect the property rights of nondomiciliaries. To do so would amount to a due process violation. Support orders are a property right. Consequently, while a state may possess the right to alter a domiciliary's marital status ex parte, as Nevada did here, in so doing it cannot abrogate the support rights of the affected spouse. Affirmed.

DISSENT: (Jackson, J.) The Court reaches the Solomon-like conclusion that the Nevada decree is half-good and half-bad for Full Faith and Credit Clause purposes. If the Court is to hold the divorce valid, it must hold all incidents of the divorce equally valid.

EDITOR'S ANALYSIS: This case illustrates what has been called a "divisible divorce": a divorce in which only portions of the award are enforceable elsewhere. It is the ex parte nature of the proceeding which gives rise to the full faith and credit problems. In this case, for instance, had Mrs. Estin (P) appeared in the Nevada divorce proceeding, the entire award would have been enforceable against her because she would have voluntarily accepted the jurisdiction of the Nevada courts over her.

[For more information on divorce, see Casenote Law Outline on Criminal Procedure, Chapter 10, § III, Termination or Dissolution of Marriage by Divorce.]

NOTES:

MAY v. ANDERSON
345 U.S. 528 (1953).

NATURE OF CASE: Habeas corpus proceeding arising from a child custody dispute.

FACT SUMMARY: After May (D) and Anderson (P) separated, Anderson (P), the father, sought and was warded an ex parte divorce with full custody of the children by a Wisconsin court. Subsequently, May (D) took possession of the children in Ohio and Anderson filed a writ in habeas corpus to secure their return pursuant to the Wisconsin decree.

CONCISE RULE OF LAW: The Full Faith and Credit Clause does not require one state to give force to a custody decree granted by another state where the rendering court did not have personal jurisdiction over the contesting spouse.

FACTS: After experiencing marital trouble, May (D) the mother and Anderson (P), the father, separated with May (D) taking the couple's children from their home in Wisconsin to Ohio. Anderson (P) sought, and was granted, an ex parte divorce with actual notice served on May (D) in Ohio. The decree also awarded full custody of the children to Anderson (P). He took custody but when the children visited the mother in Ohio, she refused to give them up. Anderson (P) filed a writ of habeas corpus for their return and the Ohio court granted the writ on the basis it was compelled by full faith and credit to recognize the validity of the Wisconsin decree.

ISSUE: Does full faith and credit require one state to give force to a custody decree issued by the court of another state where the rendering court did not have personal jurisdiction over the spouse now contesting that decree?

HOLDING AND DECISION: (Burton, J.) No. Full faith and credit will not apply to a judgment of a foreign court where personal jurisdiction was required but lacking. As we have held previously, a state may grant an ex parte divorce that must be recognized everywhere but cannot decree alimony in the absence of one of the spouses. A mother's right to her children is at least as important as her right to alimony and Wisconsin was without jurisdiction to grant custody to the father without personal jurisdiction over the mother. Ohio could not recognize the Wisconsin decree since it was granted without proper jurisdiction.

DISSENT: (Jackson, J.) The Full Faith and Credit Clause, as well as 28 U.S.C. § 1738, required that Ohio recognize the Wisconsin decree unless it lacked jurisdiction. The conclusion by the Ohio courts that Wisconsin had jurisdiction has not been contested, and that is conclusive of the matter.

EDITOR'S ANALYSIS: The Supreme Court has never satisfactorily resolved the problem of multi-state custody disputes. Despite several opportunities, the court has refused to rule directly on the issue of whether full faith and credit requires recognition of sister state custody decrees. The result has been, as Justice Jackson predicted, that whichever parent has possession of the children, however obtained, can usually apply for and be granted custody notwithstanding any previous out-of-state decree to the contrary.

_____

[For more information on recognition and enforcement of custody decrees, see Casenote Law Outline on Conflict of Laws, Chapter 10, § V, Custody of Children (Including Adoption, Paternity, and Legitimacy).]

NOTES:

JOHNSON v. MUELBERGER
340 U.S. 581 (1951).

NATURE OF CASE: Petition in probate proceedings for dower interest.

FACT SUMMARY: Johnson (P) died leaving everything to his daughter by his first marriage. His third wife asserted her claim to a widow's share and the daughter, Muelberger (D), contested the claim on the basis that his divorce from wife number two was invalid.

CONCISE RULE OF LAW: When a divorce cannot be attacked for lack of jurisdiction by parties actually before the rendering court or strangers in the rendering state then it cannot be so attacked in any other state as well.

FACTS: After the death of his first wife, Johnson (P) remarried. The second marriage ended in divorce when the second wife obtained a divorce decree in Florida. Johnson, although a resident of New York, appeared in the Florida proceeding by way of attorney and contested the allegation of wrongful acts. Although the second wife had not complied with statutory residence requirements, this issue was not raised and the decree was granted. After his death, his daughter, Muelberger (D), was to receive his entire estate by will. Mrs. Johnson (P), the third wife, interposed a claim for her widow's share. Muelberger (D) contested on the ground that her father's third marriage was invalid since the Florida court lacked jurisdiction to grant the divorce from wife two.

ISSUE: Where a divorce is immune from attack for lack of jurisdiction in the rendering state, may such an attack nonetheless be made in the courts of another state?

HOLDING AND DECISION: (Reed, J.) No. Res judicata applies to issues of jurisdiction as well as to other issues on trial. Johnson and his second wife had ample opportunity to litigate the issue of jurisdiction at the time of the decree. The fact that they did not forecloses the issue from later collateral attack by either of the parties. If Muelberger is considered to be in privity with her father, then she is also bound. If she is considered to be a stranger to the proceedings, then she has no standing since, at the time of the divorce her interest in her father's property was a mere expectancy. Since Florida would not permit Muelberger to attack the decree, neither can the courts of New York allow it. The third marriage is therefore valid.

EDITOR'S ANALYSIS: Justice Frankfurter dissented in both this case and in Sherrer v. Sherrer, the preceding case. He stated that while a divorce may meet the minimum requirements to satisfy due process the jurisdictional aspects of the decree may still he attacked collaterally by either of the parties or by a third person with sufficient standing. His view has not been followed, rather the res judicata concept has become controlling in all states.

[For more information on effect of res judicata on nonparties to divorce decree, see Casenote Law Outline on Conflict of Laws, Chapter 10, § III, Termination or Dissolution of Marriage by Divorce.]

NOTES:

YARBOROUGH v. YARBOROUGH
290 U.S. 202 (1933).

NATURE OF CASE: Review of child support order.

FACT SUMMARY: Sadie Yarborough (P), a sixteen-year-old girl living in South Carolina, sought child support from her father, W.A. Yarborough (D), despite an earlier decree of permanent support that had been entered against him in Georgia and which he had satisfied.

CONCISE RULE OF LAW: Child support obligations may not be relitigated in one state when a final order has been issued thereon in another state.

FACTS: W.A. Yarborough (D) was the father of Sadie Yarborough (D). W.A. (D) and his wife, who were Georgia residents, divorced. The Georgia court entered a final divorce decree, which included an amount of $1,725 as permanent child support. W.A. (D) paid this amount. Years later, Sadie (P), who was now living with her maternal grandfather in South Carolina, brought an action for child support. The court rejected W.A.'s (D) claim that the prior Georgia order barred the new claim and ordered W.A. (D) to pay $50 per month support. The Supreme Court granted review.

ISSUE: May child support obligations be relitigated in one state when a final order has been issued thereon in another state?

HOLDING AND DECISION: (Brandeis, J.) No. Child support obligations may not be relitigated in one state when a final order has been issued thereon in another state. The court of one state are bound by the Full Faith and Credit Clause to honor the final judgments of sister states. The fact that a plaintiff has changed residency to a state other than the state that issued the decree is of no moment. As long as the party raising the prior judgment as a defense has fulfilled his obligations under that judgment and has not taken up residency in the new forum state, he is entitled to rely on the prior judgment. Here, Georgia had entered a final judgment, and W.A. (D) had remained a Georgia resident. He can therefore rely on the conclusiveness of the Georgia judgment. Reversed.

DISSENT: (Stone, J.) There is no evidence that the Georgia judgment was intended to have extraterritorial effects. If it was, then serious constitutional questions would be raised.

EDITOR'S ANALYSIS: Spousal and, more frequently, child support orders are usually open to modification. This nonfinal aspect of such judgments has led to Full Faith and Credit Clause problems. Interlocutory judgments are often not entitled to such credit. This situation led to sufficiently serious interstate conflicts that Congress adopted legislation mandating a congressionally imposed finality for purposes of recognition.

[For more information on child support, see Casenote Law Outline on Conflict of Laws, Chapter 10, § IV, Alimony and Support.]

NOTES:

EEOC v. ARABIAN AMERICAN OIL CO.
499 U.S. 244 (1991).

NATURE OF CASE: Appeal from allowed summary judgment motion in a Title VII action.

FACT SUMMARY: Boureslan (P), a U.S. citizen working in Saudi Arabia, alleged he was discriminated against by his employer Aramco (D), a Delaware Corporation, on the grounds that he was harassed and ultimately discharged on the basis of his race, religion, and national origin.

CONCISE RULE OF LAW: It is only when Congress, in the language of the act at issue, has clearly expressed an affirmative intention to extend coverage beyond places of United States sovereignty that it will be so extended.

FACTS: Boureslan (P), a U.S. citizen, was hired by Aramco (D), a Delaware corporation, as an engineer in Houston. He was subsequently transferred to Saudi Arabia. Boureslan (P) filed a charge with the EEOC alleging discrimination and sued Armaco (D) in the United States District Court for the Southern District of Texas under Title VII, on the grounds that he was harassed and ultimately discharged by the Defendant on the basis of his race, religion, and national origin. Armaco (D) filed a motion for summary judgment on the grounds that the district court lacked subject-matter jurisdiction because the protections of Title VII do not extend to United States citizens employed abroad by American employers. The district court agreed and dismissed Boureslan's (P) claim. The Fifth Circuit affirmed. The Supreme Court granted certiorari.

ISSUE: Does Title VII apply extraterritorially to regulate the employment practices of United States employers who employ United States citizens abroad?

HOLDING AND DECISION: (Rehnquist, J.) No. Title VII does not apply extraterritorially to regulate the employment practices of United States employers who employ United States citizens abroad. Congress has the authority to enforce its laws beyond the territorial boundaries of the United States. Legislation of Congress is meant to apply only within the territorial jurisdiction of the United States unless a contrary intent appears. Language in Title VII gives no indication of Congressional purpose to extend its coverage beyond places of United States sovereignty. Evidence produced by the Plaintiff in this case fell short of demonstrating the affirmative Congressional intent required to extend the protections of Title VII beyond U.S. territorial borders. Contrary to Boureslan's (P) argument that the statute's definitions of the jurisdictional terms "employer" and "commerce" are sufficiently broad to include U.S. firms that employ American citizens oversees, the statute's definitions were ambiguous and did not speak directly to legislating extraterritorially. The intent of Congress had to be deduced by inference from boilerplate language which could be found in any number of Congressional Acts, none of which had ever been held to apply oversees. On the other hand, language like "all commerce which may lawfully be regulated by Congress" would be considered to apply abroad because it is not limited boilerplate language. Furthermore, the statute's alien exemption clause does not imply that Congress intended to protect American citizens from employment discrimination abroad because there is no way to distinguish application between United States' employers and foreign employers. In addition, other elements in the statute suggest a domestic focus. The statute speaks of states and not foreign nations and contains no mechanisms for oversees enforcement ,or for what to do when there are conflicts with the laws of other nations. Affirmed.

DISSENT: (Marshall, J., Blackmun, J., and Stevens, J.) The canon that the legislation of Congress, unless a contrary intent appears, is meant to apply only within the territorial jurisdiction of the United States is not a clear statement rule which relieves the court of the duty to give effect to all indications of the legislature's will. Rather, a court may properly rely on this presumption only after it has looked at all the traditional law that demonstrates when unexpressed Congressional intent may be ascertained. When it does in this case, it is clear that Congress did intend Title VII to protect United States citizens from discrimination by U.S. employers operating oversees. For example, the inference arising from the alien-exemption provision is more than sufficient to rebut the presumption against extraterritoriality.

EDITOR'S ANALYSIS: This is an example of the courts, in this case the highest Court of the land, being unwilling to impose law where Congress has not.

LAURITZEN v. LARSEN
345 U.S. 571 (1953).

NATURE OF CASE: Review of award of damages for personal injury.

FACT SUMMARY: Larsen (P), a Danish seaman on a Danish ship, contended that the Jones Act provided him a U.S. forum for litigating a personal injury claim arising outside the United States.

CONCISE RULE OF LAW: The Jones Act does not provide a U.S. forum to foreign seamen for injuries occurring outside the United States.

FACTS: Larsen (P), a Danish citizen temporarily residing in New York, signed on as a crew member of the Randa, a Danish ship. While in port in Cuba, he was injured. He later brought a personal injury action under the Jones Act in federal district court in New York. The court awarded him $4,267.50. The Second Circuit affirmed, and the Supreme Court granted review to determine whether the Jones Act provided foreign seamen a U.S. forum to litigate a case arising out of an injury which occurred outside the United States.

ISSUE: Does the Jones Act provide a U.S. forum to foreign seamen for injuries occurring outside the United States?

HOLDING AND DECISION: (Jackson, J.) No. The Jones Act does not provide a U.S. forum to foreign seamen for injuries occurring outside the United States. Read literally, the language of the Act would give a U.S. forum to "any seaman" who suffers personal injury within the course of his employment. However, this language must be read in the context of the body of maritime law that preceded it. By usage dating back to at least 1790, most laws dealing with admiralty give no evidence that Congress intended a foreign application, and courts have so construed them. It is not hard to see why this is so. Multiply such extraterritorial effect by the number of seagoing nations and the potential for conflict becomes obvious. This is not to say that the United States can never be a forum for a foreign national. However, for this to occur, the United States would have to have the strongest interest in the matter. Factors in this assessment include place of the tort, the law of the flag, allegiance of the injured, the allegiance of the shipowner, the place of contract, and accessibility of a foreign forum. Here, a weighing of these factors leads to the conclusion that Denmark had the greater interest. Therefore, larsen (P) had no action under the Jones Act. Reversed.

EDITOR'S ANALYSIS: Generally speaking, the trend in the law over this century has been to extend the extraterritorial reach of U.S. law. Formerly, U.S. law generally stopped at its waters' edge. Today, many federal laws quite explicitly have foreign effect. Antitrust law and certain securities laws are examples of this.

[For more information on the most significant relationship principle for tort jurisdiction, see Casenote Law Outline on Conflict of Laws, Chapter 6, § II, Modern Approaches.]

NOTES:

HARTFORD FIRE INSURANCE CO. v. CALIFORNIA
113 S. Ct. 2891 (1993).

NATURE OF CASE: Consolidated review of orders granting motions to dismiss complaints brought under the Sherman Act for illegal restraint of trade.

FACT SUMMARY: When nineteen states (P) sued domestic and foreign insurance companies (D) for conspiring to limit the availability of insurance coverage, the foreign companies (D) moved to dismiss on the ground of international comity, arguing that their conduct was permissible under British law.

CONCISE RULE OF LAW: A district court should not decline to exercise jurisdiction on the grounds of international comity where there is no true conflict between domestic and foreign law.

FACTS: Hartford (D) was a primary insurer offering commercial general liability coverage to consumers in California (P). London reinsurers (D) sought changes in the standard commercial insurance policies offered by Hartford (D) to consumers to limit claims. The changes had the effect of making "occurrence" coverage unavailable, especially coverage for pollution-related risks. California (P) sued the insurance companies (D) in federal district court for illegal restraint of trade under the Sherman Act. The insurance companies (D) moved to dismiss for failure to state a cause of action. The London reinsurers (D) contended that the district court should refrain from exercising jurisdiction because of international comity; the conduct complained of was permissible under British law and the interests of Britain were such that applying the Sherman Act would conflict significantly with British law. The District Court granted the motion, and California (P) appealed. The Court of Appeals reversed, and the Supreme Court granted review.

ISSUE: Should a district court decline to exercise jurisdiction on the grounds of international comity where there is no true conflict between domestic and foreign law?

HOLDING AND DECISION: (Souter, J.) No. A district court should not decline to exercise jurisdiction on the grounds of international comity where there is no true conflict between domestic and foreign law. In this case, the London reinsurers (D) contend that applying the Sherman Act to their conduct would conflict significantly with British law. They assert that Parliament has established a comprehensive regulatory regime over the London reinsurance market and that the conduct alleged here was perfectly consistent with British law and policy. But this is not the same as stating a conflict. Since the London reinsurers (D) do not argue that British law requires them to act in some fashion prohibited by the law of the United States or claim that their compliance with the laws of both countries is otherwise impossible, there is no conflict with British law. Affirmed.

DISSENT: (Scalia, J.) There is clearly a conflict in this case. The reinsurers (D) were not compelled by British law to take their allegedly wrongful actions, but that does not preclude a conflict-of-laws analysis. Where applicable foreign and domestic law provide different substantive rules of decision to govern the parties' dispute, a conflict-of-laws analysis is necessary.

EDITOR'S ANALYSIS: The majority was clearly concerned, as was the court of appeals, about the London reinsurers' (D) express purpose to affect U.S. commerce and the substantial nature of the effect produced. The Court was not going to allow the London reinsurers (D) to hide behind comity when the interest of the United States was so significant. Yet, in that sense, the Court is making a choice to implement one law over another.

[For more information on comity, see Casenote Law Outline on Conflict of Laws, Chapter 9, § III, Collateral Estoppel and Full Faith and Credit.]

NOTES:

FILARTIGA v. PENA-IRALA
577 F. Supp. 860 (E.D.N.Y. 1984).

NATURE OF CASE: Action for damages under 28 U.S.C. § 1350.

FACT SUMMARY: The Filartigas (P), suing a former Paraguayan official for acts of torture and murder, contended that damages should be measured by reference to international law.

CONCISE RULE OF LAW: The measure of damages recoverable under 28 U.S.C. § 1350 may be determined by reference to international law.

FACTS: The Filartigas (P), Paraguayan nationals and brother and son of decedent Joelito Filartiga, brought an action against Pena (D) in federal district court under 28 U.S.C. § 1350. They alleged that Pena (D), in his capacity as a high police official in Asuncion, Paraguay, had tortured and murdered Joelito for antigovernment activities. The district court dismissed for lack of jurisdiction, but the court of appeals reversed. A federal magistrate, applying Paraguayan tort law, recommended a damage award of $375,000. Joel (P) and Dolly (P) Filartiga objected to this amount. The district court undertook a de novo review.

ISSUE: May the measure of damages recoverable under 28 U.S.C. § 1350 be determined by reference to international law?

HOLDING AND DECISION: (Nickerson, J.) Yes. The measure of damages recoverable under 28 U.S.C. § 1350 may be determined by reference to international law. Under 28 U.S.C. § 1350, the district courts have jurisdiction over a civil actin by an alien for a tort committed in violation of the law of nations or a U.S. treaty. Nothing in either the language or purpose of the section would tend to limit damages awardable thereunder to the law of any particular state. To so hold would eviscerate the section by allowing individual states to enact immunities for acts objectionable under international law. When the laws of an affected state are consistent with international law, they may be looked to for a measure of damages; when not, they need not be. Here, torture and murder are against Paraguayan law. However, Paraguay does not afford exemplary damages for torts. Given the abominable nature of Pena's (D) acts, punitive damages, which are awardable under international law, are appropriate in this case. [The court went on to enter a total judgment of $10,385,364.]

EDITOR'S ANALYSIS: Prior to 1991, § 1350 was not always interpreted as expansively as it was here. Numerous courts, viewing "the law of nations" as referring only to acts that dealt with international relations, would not extend jurisdiction to acts by officials against their own countrymen. Changes made in 1991 put official acts of torture specifically within the law's ambit.

[For more information on choice of law theories, see Casenote Law Outline on Conflict of Laws, Chapter 5, § VII, Selecting a Choice-of-Law Theory.]

NOTES:

UNITED STATES v. YUNIS

681 F. Supp. 896 (D.D.C. 1988).

NATURE OF CASE: Motion to dismiss various indictments in prosecution for hostage taking and airline hijacking.

FACT SUMMARY: Yunis (D) contended that he could not be prosecuted by the Government (P) for a hijacking that he perpetrated when its only connection to the United States was that several Americans were aboard.

CONCISE RULE OF LAW: An airline hijacker may be prosecuted by the federal government even if the hijacking's only connection with the United States was the presence of Americans on board.

FACTS: Yunis (D) and several accomplices hijacked a Jordanian airliner while it was on the ground in Beirut. It flew to several locations around the Mediterranean Sea, and eventually flew back to Beirut, where the hijackers blew up the plane and then escaped into the hills. The only connection between the entire episode and the United States was that several Americans were on board the whole time. Yunis (D) was indicted for violating the Hostage Taking Act, 18 U.S.C. § 1203. He was apprehended, and later indicted under the Destruction of Aircraft Act, 18 U.S.C. § 32. He moved to dismiss on jurisdictional grounds.

ISSUE: May an airline hijacker be prosecuted by the federal government even if the hijacking's only connection with the United States was that several Americans were aboard?

HOLDING AND DECISION: (Parker, J.) Yes. An airline hijacker may be prosecuted by the federal government even if the hijacking's only connection with the United States was that several Americans were aboard. For jurisdiction in such a situation to exist, there must be jurisdiction under both international and domestic law. International law relates to the power of Congress to have extraterritorial application of its law; domestic law relates to its intent to do so. International law recognizes several bases for a nation to give extraterritorial application to its laws. One is the "universal principle." Some acts are considered to be so heinous and contrary to civilization that any court may assert jurisdiction. What acts fall within this category are largely defined by international convention. Numerous conventions condemn hijacking and hostage taking, so the universal principle applies. Also relevant is the "passive personal principle," which applies to offenses against a nation's citizens abroad. While the United States has been slow to recognize this principle, it is now generally agreed upon. International law having been disposed of on this issue, domestic law must now be discussed. The Hostage Taking Act, at subsection (b)(1)(A), clearly includes an offender that has seized or detained a U.S. citizen. The language could not be plainer. As to the Destruction of Aircraft Act, it appears from the language of the Act and the Federal Aviation Act, 18 U.S.C. § 31, that the law was intended to apply only when the aircraft in question either began or ended its flight in the United States. Since the flight in question did not do this, the Act does not apply. Motion denied in part; granted in part.

EDITOR'S ANALYSIS: Three other generally accepted bases for jurisdiction exist. These are territorial (jurisdiction over territory), national (jurisdiction over a person) and protective (jurisdiction necessary to protect a state.) Of the five generally recognized jurisdictional grounds, the passive personal principle has been the one to meet with the most resistance by U.S. courts and officials.

_____

[For more information on federal jurisdiction in international cases, see Casenote Law Outline on Conflict of Laws, Chapter 4, § IV, Federal Common Law.]

NOTES:

UNITED STATES v. VERDUGO-URQUIDEZ
856 F.2d 1214 (9th Cir. 1988).

NATURE OF CASE: Appeal from order suppressing evidence in a narcotics prosecution of a foreign national.

FACT SUMMARY: The Government (P), prosecuting Verdugo-Urquidez (D), a Mexican, for narcotics violations, contended that the Fourth Amendment did not apply to foreign nationals arrested outside the United States.

CONCISE RULE OF LAW: The Fourth Amendment applies to foreign nationals arrested outside the United States.

FACTS: The Government (P) suspected that Verdugo-Urquidez (D), a Mexican national living in Mexico, of being a drug kingpin. At the request of the Drug Enforcement Agency, Verdugo-Urquidez (D) was arrested and turned over at the border to DEA officials. DEA officials then, with the cooperation of Mexican officials, searched his two residences. Incriminating evidence was found. Indicted on numerous narcotics violation counts, Verdugo-Urquidez (D) moved to suppress. The motion was granted. The Government (P) appealed, contending that the Fourth Amendment did not apply to foreign nationals arrested outside U.S. territory.

ISSUE: Does the Fourth Amendment apply to foreign nationals arrested outside U.S. territory?

HOLDING AND DECISION: (Thompson, J.) Yes. The Fourth Amendment applies to foreign nationals arrested outside U.S. territory. It must be remembered that the Government (P) obtains its existence solely from the Constitution, having no life apart from it. Its powers and limitations are found therein. The principal argument against application of the Constitution to noncitizens is that it is a contract between U.S. citizens and the federal government, and foreigners are not parties to that contract. However, for various reasons this is not a valid view of constitutional analysis. Historically, the founders of this nation had great respect for "natural rights," and such rights were incident to status as human beings, not status as citizens. Further, the Supreme Court has, in numerous decisions, extended constitutional protections to aliens, both legal and illegal. If the Court is willing to extend constitutional protections to those here illegally, it is only logical to extend them to one such as Verdugo-Urquidez (D), who is here not illegally but rather due to government action. Therefore, the conclusion must be that the Fourth Amendment provides protection to foreign nationals arrested outside U.S. territory. [The court then discussed the merits and affirmed.]

DISSENT: (Wallace, J.) That a nonresident alien has any reasonable expectation of privacy, for Fourth Amendment purposes, in his foreign country with respect to our government is a ludicrous proposition. Beyond this, the preamble itself, "we the people of the United States..." provides all the textual basis necessary for no extraterritorial application of constitutional protections.

EDITOR'S ANALYSIS: This case eventually made its way to the Supreme Court. The Court in United States v. Verdugo-Urquidez, 494 U.S. 259 (1990), held the Fourth Amendment inapplicable. Two years later, the Court rendered an opinion regarding an alleged associate of Verdugo-Urquidez (D). In a controversial decision, the Court held that the U.S. could exercise jurisdiction over a foreign national who had been kidnapped abroad and brought to the United States for trial, despite the existence of an extradition treaty between the United States and the government of the nation where the U.S.-authorized kidnapping was committed. (United States v. Alvarez Machain, U.S. 112 S.Ct. 2188 (1992).

[For more information on constitutional limits on international cases, see Casenote Law Outline on Conflict of Laws, Chapter 3, § V, Special Problems.]

NOTES:

UNITED STATES v. DAVIS
905 F.2d 245 (9th Cir. 1989).

NATURE OF CASE: Appeal from convictions for possession of, and conspiracy to possess marijuana, with the intent to distribute, in violation of the Maritime Drug Law Enforcement Act.

FACT SUMMARY: Davis (D), a non-U.S. citizen, was apprehended by the Coast Guard on the high seas for possessing, and conspiring to possess with the intent to distribute, 7,000 pounds of marijuana.

CONCISE RULE OF LAW: The provisions of the Maritime Drug Law Enforcement Act apply to persons in foreign vessels outside the territory of the United States.

FACTS: A Coast Guard boat encountered a sailboat about 35 miles off the coast of California headed toward San Francisco. Davis (D), not a citizen of the U.S., denied the Coast Guard's request to board, alleging it had no authority because the boat was of British registry and was sailing on the high seas en route to the Caribbean via Mexico from Hong Kong. The Coast Guard suspected Davis's boat of smuggling contraband and requested permission from the United Kingdom to board in accordance with an agreement between the U.S. and the U.K. The U.K. gave the U.S. permission. By the time the Coast Guard boarded, the boat was approximately 100 miles west of the California coast. The boarding officer smelled marijuana and saw numerous bales of material when he went below deck with Davis (D) to retrieve Davis's gun. The Coast Guard arrested Davis (D), brought the boat to an island off San Francisco, and confiscated 7,000 pounds of marijuana. Davis (D) filed a motion to dismiss for lack of jurisdiction and a motion to suppress evidence obtained from his boat. The district court denied both motions. Davis (D) appealed, contending that the provisions of the Maritime Drug Law Enforcement Act do not apply to persons in foreign vessels outside the territory of the United States.

ISSUE: Does Congress have the authority to give extraterritorial effect to the Maritime Drug Law Enforcement Act, and is the Act constitutionally applied to a Defendant who is in a foreign vessel outside the territory of the United States?

HOLDING AND DECISION: (Wiggins, J.) Yes. Congress has the authority to give extraterritorial effect to the Act. The Constitution doesn't prohibit the U.S. from punishing Davis's (D) conduct. The Constitution authorized Congress to give extraterritorial effect to the Act because Congress has the power, based on the Constitution, to define and punish piracies and felonies on the high seas. Congress has explicitly stated that it intended the Maritime Drug Law Enforcement Act to apply extraterritorially. Furthermore, a sufficient nexus exists so that the application of the Maritime Drug Law Enforcement Act to Davis's extraterritorial conduct does not violate the Due Process clause because there was an attempted transaction which was aimed at causing criminal acts within the United States. Possession and conspiracy to posses with the intent to distribute on board a vessel is subject to U.S. jurisdiction. Foreign vessels subject to U.S. jurisdiction are those located within the custom waters of the U.S., custom waters being ones where vessels are subject to a treaty or an arrangement between a foreign government and the U.S. The United States obtained permission from the U.K. to board, search, and seize the vessel in accordance with an agreement between the two countries. That permission constitutes an arrangement. The Coast Guard had reasonable suspicion to believe the boat was importing drugs. The protections of the fourth amendment do not extend to the search of Davis's (D) boat on the high seas. Affirmed.

EDITOR'S ANALYSIS: This case is an example of the court's willingness to apply a law extraterritorially when there was permission from a foreign citizen's government to do so.

MATUSEVITCH v. IVANOVICH
877 F. SUPP. 1 (D.D.C. 1995).

NATURE OF CASE: Motion for summary judgment to not enforce a foreign judgment.

FACT SUMMARY: Telnikoff sought to have a judgment acquired in Britain enforced in federal court in Maryland. Matusevitch (P) moved to have the foreign judgment deemed unenforceable.

CONCISE RULE OF LAW: When foreign libel standards are contrary to U.S. libel standards, so much so that they would be repugnant to the public policies of the state of Maryland and of the United States, the foreign judgment will not be recognized.

FACTS: Matusevitch (P), presently a Maryland resident, while working in Europe wrote a letter in 1984 to a London newspaper regarding cross-border radio broadcast to Russia. The letter accused Telnikoff of racism. Telnikoff won a libel judgment against Matusevitch (P) in Britain and sought to have the judgment enforced in federal court in Maryland. Matusevitch (P) moved to have the judgment deemed unenforceable in the U.S.

ISSUE: Will the foreign judgment be recognized and enforced in a Maryland federal court?

HOLDING AND DECISION: (Urbina, J.) No. The foreign judgment will not be recognized and enforced in the U.S. because the foreign libel standards are repugnant to the public policy of Maryland. Per a Maryland statute, foreign judgments will not be recognized if the cause of action on which the judgment is based is repugnant to Maryland public policy. Furthermore, comity doesn't require, but forbids, recognition when such recognition works a direct violation of the policy of Maryland laws; for example, when such judgments are incongruent with First Amendment protections. Here the differences in the laws are so great that they are repugnant to Maryland and U.S. libel law. In British libel law, the plaintiff is not required to prove that the statements were false, and the defendant's state of mind and intentions are also not considered. Enforcement in the U.S. would, therefore, deprive the Plaintiff of his constitutional rights because those considerations are elements of U.S. libel law. Moreover, the speech at is issue is protected under the First Amendment and thereby inactionable in U.S. Courts. In addition, the statements were merely opinions, not fact. Furthermore, the Defendant was a limited public figure and had to show the Plaintiff acted with malice, something he wasn't required to do in Britain but would have had to do in the U.S. Summary judgment was therefore granted in favor of Matusevitch (P).

EDITOR'S ANALYSIS: When the differences between U.S. law and foreign law are only minor differences in statutory law and rules of civil procedure or corporate or commercial law, the foreign judgment will most likely be enforced.

126

STARMEDIA NETWORK, INC. v. STAR MEDIA INC.
2001 U.S. Dist. LEXIS 4870 (S.D.N.Y. 2001).

NATURE OF CASE: Motion to dismiss a trademark infringement action for lack of personal jurisdiction.

FACT SUMMARY: Starmedia (P) sued Star Media (D) for infringement of its domain and corporate name trademark rights.

CONCISE RULE OF LAW: If a nonresident has sufficient minimum contacts with a jurisdiction, and it is not unreasonable for that jurisdiction to exercise jurisdiction, then it is appropriate for a nonresident to have to litigate in a foreign jurisdiction.

FACTS: Starmedia (P), a Delaware corporation with a principal place of business in New York, sued Star Media (D), a Washington corporation, for infringement of its domain and corporate name trademark rights. Starmedia (P) provides a variety of information and services, including a portal in the Spanish and Portuguese languages. Star Media (D) is a wholesale seller of software. Star Media's (D) website is interactive and includes a chart of shipping costs by U.S. time zones. Customers can use the site to send comments to defendants, and dealer applications can be downloaded. In addition, registered users, via a password, can obtain information regarding products and pricing. Star Media (D) has stipulated that it receives substantial revenue from international commerce, that it solicits business nationwide via the website, and that one of the purposes of the website is to attract new customers from New York. No goods have been sold in New York, however. Star Media (D) has two employees and two hundred customers. When Star Media (D) registered its website name, it knew that the plaintiff's website existed. Star Media (D) moved to dismiss for lack of personal jurisdiction.

ISSUE: Does Star Media (D) have sufficient contacts with New York that make the exercise of personal jurisdiction appropriate and reasonable?

HOLDING AND DECISION: (Cote, J.) Yes. Star Media (D) has sufficient contacts with New York that make the exercise of personal jurisdiction both appropriate and reasonable. The level and nature of the information exchanged on Star Media's (D) website rises to the level of an interactive website which permits the exchange of information between Star Media (D) and website viewers, although the level of interactivity is limited. The website does not involve the actual conduct of business, but the site is commercial in nature. Customers can see confidential information and communicate via e-mail. No on-line orders are taken, and products aren't sold over the Internet. Star Media (D), however, had additional contacts with New York, which make it reasonable to confer personal jurisdiction. Star Media (D) knew of plaintiff's domain name prior to registering its own. It therefore should have anticipated being hailed into the forum of Plaintiff's principal place of business, New York, to answer to any allegation. In addition, Star Media (D) derived income from interstate commerce and used the website to support its sales, including potentially gaining New York customers. Sufficient minimum contacts have, therefore, been established. It is reasonable to exercise jurisdiction because the Defendant has offered no evidence to prove any particular hardship by having to litigate in New York. Defendant's motion is denied.

EDITOR'S ANALYSIS: Unlike in *Cybersell,* Star Media (D) had purposefully availed itself of New York's forum by having more than mere knowledge that its website may appear in another state.

CAESARS WORLD INC. v. CAESARS-PALACE.COM
112 F.Supp. 2d 502 (E.D. Va. 2000).

NATURE OF CASE: Motion to dismiss a domain infringement action.

FACT SUMMARY: Caesars (P) brought an action against many domain names, alleging violations of the Lanham Act and its amendment, the Anticybersquatting Consumer Protection Act.

CONCISE RULE OF LAW: In rem jurisdiction over defendants who are not subject to the personal jurisdiction of any court does not violate the due process standards under the Constitution.

FACTS: Caesars (P) brought an action against a multitude of domain names, alleging violations of the Anticybersquatting Act. The Anticybersquatting Act allows for an in rem proceeding by the owner of a mark against a domain name, in the judicial district in which the domain name register is located, if the name violated any right of the owner of a registered mark, and if that owner is not able to obtain in personam jurisdiction over an allowed defendant. The Defendants moved to dismiss the action, alleging that the complaint would violate their due process rights if the court exercised in rem jurisdiction. The motion was denied.

ISSUE: Does in rem jurisdiction over defendants who are not subject to the personal jurisdiction of the Anticybersquatting Act meet the due process standards under the Constitution?

HOLDING AND DECISION: (Bryan, J.) Yes. In rem jurisdiction over defendants who are not subject to the personal jurisdiction of the Anticybersquatting Act meets the due process standards under the Constitution. Given the limited relief offered by the Act, no due process violation occurs here as to Defendants personally. Furthermore, there is no prohibition on a legislative body's making something property, such as domain name. It is unnecessary for minimum contacts personal jurisdiction standards to be applied because the property, that is, the domain name, is not only related to the cause of action but is its entire subject matter. Moreover, to the extent that minimum contacts are required for in rem jurisdiction, the fact that a domain name was registered with a Virginia company supplies that. Caesars (P) motion was denied.

EDITOR'S ANALYSIS: By the legislature defining a domain name as a tangible piece of property, another avenue of jurisdiction is open to plaintiffs.

CASPI v. THE MICROSOFT NETWORK, LLC
732 A.2d 528 (N.J. App. 1999).

NATURE OF CASE: Appeal of a motion to dismiss based on a forum selection clause in a breach of contract and fraud action.

FACT SUMMARY: This is a class action by members (P) of the Microsoft Network against Microsoft, LLC (D) for breach of contract and fraud.

CONCISE RULE OF LAW: A forum selection clause is valid if it can be shown that there was no fraud or overweening bargaining power, that the clause doesn't contravene public policy, and that the parties agreeing to it were put on notice.

FACTS: Caspi (P) brought a class action on behalf of one and half million members of the Microsoft Network, an Internet service provider, against the Microsoft Network, LLC (D) for breach of contract and fraud. Microsoft (D) moved to dismiss on the basis of a forum selection clause in the Microsoft Network membership agreement. The clause read, "This agreement is governed by the laws of the State of Washington, USA, and you consent to the exclusive jurisdiction and venue of courts in King County, Washington in all disputes arising out of or relating to your use of MSN or your MSN membership." The trial judge allowed the motion. Caspi (P) appealed.

ISSUE: Is the forum selection clause valid?

HOLDING AND DECISION: (Kestin, J.) Yes. The forum selection clause is valid because there is no evidence of fraud or overweening bargaining power, the clause did not contravene public policy, and the Plaintiffs had notice of it. The clause does not lack clarity. The clause was reasonable, clear, and contained no material misrepresentations. Therefore, the clause doesn't constitute fraud. Furthermore, the inclusion of a forum selection in a consumer contract does not in itself constitute overweening bargaining power. Something more than merely size difference must be shown. In this case, there was no evidence of an imbalance in size which resulted in an inequality of bargaining power that was unfairly exploited by Microsoft (D). Moreover, Caspi (P) had other services available, but Caspi (P) chose to agree to the clause. Furthermore, the nature of the protections afforded by the State of Washington are not materially different, or less broad in scope, than those available in New Jersey. Lastly, the Plaintiffs received adequate notice of the clause through an electronic medium and were free to scroll through the various computer screens that presented the terms of their contracts before clicking their agreement. There was also nothing extraordinary about the size or the placement of the clause's text. Affirmed.

EDITOR'S ANALYSIS: Generally, forum selection clauses are considered valid and are enforced by the courts.

AMERICA ONLINE, INC. v. SUPERIOR COURT OF ALAMEDA COUNTY
90 Cal. App. 4th 1, 108 Cal. Rptr. 2d 699 (1st App. Cal. 2001).

NATURE OF CASE: Appeal of denied motion to dismiss in an action based on violations of the California Unfair Business Practices Act, conversion, and fraud.

FACT SUMMARY: Former subscribers (P) to America Online (D) filed a class action against America (D) for violation of the California Unfair Business Act, conversion, and fraud.

CONCISE RULE OF LAW: Forum selection clauses are honored if they are procured freely and voluntarily, with the place chosen having some logical nexus to one of the parties or to the dispute, and so long as California consumers will not find their substantial legal rights significantly impaired by its enforcement.

FACTS: Former subscribers (P) to America Online (D) filed a class action against the company alleging that America (D) continued to debit the Plaintiffs' credit cards for monthly service fees after termination of their subscription. The subscribers (P) alleged conversion, fraud, and a violation of the California Unfair Business Practices Act. America (D) filed a motion to dismiss based on a forum selection clause contained in America's (D) on-line "Terms of Service Agreement", which clause designated Virginia as the forum. The agreement also contained a choice of law provision designating Virginia has the chosen law. The district court denied the motion to dismiss, and America (D) appealed.

ISSUE: Should the forum selection clause at issue in this case be enforced?

HOLDING AND DECISION: (Ruvolo, J.) No. The forum selection clause shouldn't be enforced because California public policy would be violated in that the rights of California consumers would be significantly impaired. If the action were heard in Virginia, Virginia substantive law would be applied, and the application of that law would materially diminish the rights of California residents. The California Unfair Business Practices Act is a legislative embodiment of a desire to protect California consumers and furthers strong public policy of California. Enforcement of the forum selection clause would necessitate a waiver of the statutory remedies the California Act provides and would violate the Act's antiwaiver provision and California public policy. In addition, Virginia provides far less consumer protection to its citizens than California provides to its own, such as hostility to class actions. Moreover, neither punitive damages nor enhanced remedies are available for disabled and senior citizens in Virginia. In addition, in Virginia reduced recovery is mandated for unintentional acts, there is a shorter period of limitations, and the state uses a Lodestar formula to calculate attorney fees. Costs and convenience are not to be included in the test for reasonableness of forum selection clauses. Affirmed.

EDITOR'S ANALYSIS: Unlike in *Caspi*, this court considered the choice of law provision in the agreement, in addition to the forum selection clause, and focused on the substantive law differences between the two states, not on whether the plaintiff received notice of the terms of the agreement. Unlike in *Caspi*, public policy interests were violated here because the substantive law of the two states were very different and less favorable to the plaintiff in Virginia than in California.

AMERICA ONLINE, INC. v. NATIONAL HEALTH CARE DISCOUNT, INC.
121 F. Supp. 2d 1255 (D. Iowa 2000).

NATURE OF CASE: Analysis by the court to determine which state law applies.

FACT SUMMARY: National (D) sent a large volume of unsolicited bulk e-mail to millions of America (P) users causing a great expense to America (P). America (P) sued.

CONCISE RULE OF LAW: When there is no clearly demonstrated place where the alleged conduct underlying the cause of action occurred, the law of the state where the injury occurred is the law that will be used.

FACTS: America (P), a Delaware corporation with a principal place of business in Virginia, sued National (D), an Iowa corporation with an administrative office in Iowa and sales offices in Georgia, Missouri, Arizona, Texas and Denver, for conversion, trespass, unjust enrichment, and violations of various state and federal statutes. National (D) is in the business of selling discount optical and dental service plans. Using contract e-mailers from all over the country, National (D) solicited business through large-volume, unsolicited bulk e-mail. Millions of these messages went to America (P) users at great expense to America (P).

ISSUE: Should the law of the state where the injury occurred be used when there is no clearly demonstrated place where the alleged conduct occurred?

HOLDING AND DECISION: (Zoss, J.) Yes. According to Iowa choice-of-law rules, Virginia law shall apply because there was no clearly demonstrated place where the alleged conduct occurred, but the place where the injury occurred was Virginia. Iowa follows the "most significant relationship" test as expressed in the Restatement which dictates that the relevant policies of Iowa and Virginia are to be considered. Although Iowa has an interest in the regulation of the actions of corporations doing business in Iowa, the only actions by National (D) in Iowa were incorporation of the entity, maintenance of an office, and issuance of checks to pay contract e-mailers. All the actions giving rise to the lawsuit appear to have occurred elsewhere, in a number of different states. In addition to regulating the conduct of persons within its territory, a state also has an obvious interest in providing redress for injuries that occurred there. In this instant case, because there is no clearly demonstrated place where the alleged conduct occurred, the law of the place where the injury occurred, which is Virginia, will be used. Virginia is the site of America's (P) hardware that it alleges was overburdened by National (D), and it is also the place where America (P) allegedly sustained its economic loss.

EDITOR'S ANALYSIS: Although no state has a clear relationship to the events giving rise to this action, Virginia's relationship appears to be the most significant.

LICRA ET UEJF v. YAHOO! INC.

Antiracist group (P) v. Internet service provider (D)

Tribunal de Grande Instance de Paris, May 22, 2000.

NATURE OF CASE: Action for damages for internet site's violation of French penal law.

FACT SUMMARY: The French League Against Racism and Antisemitism (LICRA) and the Jewish Students' Union of France (P) sued Yahoo (D) because its website, Yahoo.com, included an auction page offering Nazi relics and flags for sale, in contravention of French criminal law.

CONCISE RULE OF LAW: Where a website points toward sites, pages or forums that would likely be considered criminal or an illegal nuisance, it must warn surfers, by a banner, prior to entry to the site, to interrupt visiting that site to avoid sanctions under French law.

FACTS: Yahoo! Inc. (D) operated the Yahoo.com website which was accessible in France. LICRA (P) sued to prevent the sale of Nazi memorabilia through a Yahoo (D) auction page, claiming the sale of Nazi objects constituted a violation of French law.

ISSUE: Where a website points toward sites, pages or forums that would likely be considered criminal or an illegal nuisance, must it warn surfers, by a banner, prior to entry to the site, to interrupt visiting that site to avoid sanctions under French law?

HOLDING AND DECISION: (C.J.) Yes. Where a website points toward sites, pages or forums that would likely be considered criminal or an illegal nuisance, it must warn surfers, by a banner, prior to entry to the site, to interrupt visiting that site to avoid sanctions under French law. Yahoo (D) has two months to formulate proposals of technical measures likely to lead to settlement of this dispute. LICRA (P) is awarded damages and costs.

EDITOR'S ANALYSIS: Yahoo (D) claimed that it did not have the technological means to block access to specific websites. A panel of specialists was later appointed to investigate. A similar case in Germany, involving illegal pornographic websites, ended when the German Parliament enacted legislation holding internet providers liable only if they were aware of the content and failed to use technologically possible and reasonable means to block it.

QUICKNOTES

AUCTION - A public sale accomplished by means of competitive bidding.

NOTES:

AMERICAN LIBRARY ASSOCIATION v. PATAKI
969 F. Supp. 160 (S.D.N.Y. 1997).

NATURE OF CASE: Action alleging that the dormant Commerce Clause is violated by a New York law.

FACT SUMMARY: Action by American (P) against Pataki (D) alleging that the dormant Commerce Clause is violated by a New York law.

CONCISE RULE OF LAW: The Commerce Clause is violated when a state imposes its laws on citizens of another state who didn't intentionally reach out to the other state, when a state's law imposes excessive burdens on interstate commerce in relation to the local benefits it confers, and when a single state attempts to regulate a broad issue that requires national regulation.

FACTS: American (P) is a group of individuals and organizations who use the Internet to communicate, disseminate, display, and access a broad range of communications. The communications are made and are accessible both within and outside New York. American (P) has sued Pataki (D), the Governor of New York, alleging that N.Y. Penal Law § 235.21 violates the dormant Commerce Clause.

ISSUE: Is the Commerce Clause violated by the New York Law?

HOLDING AND DECISION: (Preska, J.) Yes. The Commerce Clause is violated by the New York law because the law is imposed on citizens of other states when they didn't intend to act within New York borders, because the law imposes excessive burdens on interstate commerce in relation to the local benefits it confers, and because the Internet needs to be regulated nationally and not by a single state. The nature of the Internet makes it impossible to restrict the effects of the New York law to conduct occurring within New York. An Internet user may not intend that a message be accessible to New Yorkers but lacks the ability to prevent New Yorkers from visiting a particular website. Thus, conduct that may be legal in the state in which the user acts can subject the user to prosecution in New York and thus subordinate the user's home state's policy. Furthermore, the Commerce Clause is also violated because the law is an invalid, indirect regulation of interstate commerce because the law imposes excessive burdens on interstate commerce in relation to the local benefits it confers. The law can have no effect on communications originating outside the U.S., and it will be difficult to prosecute offenders who reside out of state. Therefore, its benefit is limited. Moreover, only pictorial and not text messages are a violation. Other New York laws can serve the same purpose. The benefit is also limited in that the sale of obscene material or the luring of children is not prohibited. Balanced against these limited local benefits is the extreme burden on interstate commerce. The law casts a worldwide net and has a chilling effect. Furthermore, the cost to comply would drive many users away. Lastly, the Internet needs to be regulated nationally or globally, and regulation by any single state can only result in chaos.

EDITOR'S ANALYSIS: The borderless world of the Internet raises questions concerning the relationship among the several states and the relationship of the federal government to each state. The court believes here that because there is no control of the Internet as to who receives the content someone puts on it, one shouldn't be held responsible for that content if it enters a jurisdiction that prohibits it.

WASHINGTON v. HECKEL
24 P.3d 404 (Wash. 2001).

NATURE OF CASE: Appeal from allowed motion for summary judgment in an action alleging a violation of a state's commercial electronic mail act.

FACT SUMMARY: The State of Washington (P) sued Heckel (D), an Oregon resident, alleging that his transmissions of e-mail to Washington residents violated Washington's commercial electronic mail act.

CONCISE RULE OF LAW: An act which prohibits misrepresentation of the subject line or transmission path of any commercial e-mail message sent to Washington residents or from a Washington computer unconstitutionally burdens interstate commerce.

FACTS: The State of Washington (P) sued Heckel (D), an Oregon resident, alleging that his transmissions of e-mail to Washington residents violated Washington's commercial electronic mail act (the Act). The Act provides that anyone sending a commercial e-mail message from a computer located in Washington, or to an e-mail address held by a Washington resident, may not use a third-party's domain name without permission, misrepresent or disguise in any other way the message's point of origin or transmission path, or use a misleading subject line. Heckel (D), doing business as Natural Instincts, sent 100,000 to 1,000,000 unsolicited commercial e-mails over the Internet per week. The text of the message was a lengthy sales pitch and ended with an order form for a book that the recipient could download, print, and mail to an Oregon address for Natural Instincts. Heckel (D) made 30-50 sales per month, charging $39.95 for the booklet. Washington (P) filed suit against Heckel (D) alleging that he had violated the Act by using false or misleading information in the subject line — such as "Did I get the right e-mail address?" and "For your review ___ HANDS OFF!", by misrepresenting information defining the transmission paths of his messages, by using transmission paths that were registered to other entities and could not send or receive messages, and by failing to provide a valid return e-mail address to which the bulk-mail recipients could respond. Washington (P) sought a permanent injunction, civil penalties, costs, and attorney's fees. On cross motions for summary judgment, the trial court dismissed Washington's (P) suit against Heckel (D), concluding that the Act violated the dormant Commerce Clause of the U.S. Constitution because the Act was unduly restrictive and burdensome. Washington (P) appealed.

ISSUE: Does the Act which prohibits misrepresentation of the subject line or transmission path of any commercial e-mail message sent to Washington residents or from a Washington computer unconstitutionally burden interstate commerce?

HOLDING AND DECISION: (Owens, J.) No. The Act does not unduly burden interstate commerce. The Act does not openly discriminate against interstate commerce in favor of Washington's (P) economic interest because the Act is equally enforceable against out-of-state residents as it is against in-state residents. The local benefits of the Act also surpass any alleged burden on interstate commerce. The Act protects the interests of Internet service providers, actual owners of forged domain names, and e-mail users. Internet service providers are placed with a tremendous burden when they have to handle an enormous volume of mass mailings, including trying to return e-mail to an address that does not exist. The Act protects against that burden. In addition, owners of impermissibly used domain names and e-mail addresses suffer economic harm, because they receive an enormous number of responses to mail that they have never sent out. These responses may cause damage to their computer system. The Act protects against this as well. Furthermore, the Act also protects recipients who are unable to opt out of bulk e-mail messages and who may be harmed if they have to pay for the time reading e-mail messages they think are from someone else. On the other hand, the only burden the Act places on bulk e-mailers is truthfulness in their subject line and transmission path, a requirement that does not burden commerce but actually facilitates it by eliminating fraud and deception. Also, bulk mailers do not incur a cost to comply with the Act. Furthermore, the Act survives both the inconsistency among states test and the regulating conduct wholly outside of Washington test. Seventeen other states have passed legislation regulating electronic solicitations, and the truthfulness requirements of the Act do not conflict with any of the requirements in the other states' statutes. Reversed.

EDITOR'S ANALYSIS: Unlike *American Library Association*, the court in this case found that the Act did not a violate the Commerce Clause. The Act only reaches those deceptive bulk e-mail messages directed to Washington residents or initiated from a computer in Washington and does not impose liability for messages merely routed through Washington or read by a Washington resident who was not the actual addressee. The opinion in this case came down approximately four years after *American*.

GLOSSARY
COMMON LATIN WORDS AND PHRASES ENCOUNTERED IN THE LAW

A FORTIORI: Because one fact exists or has been proven, therefore a second fact that is related to the first fact must also exist.

A PRIORI: From the cause to the effect. A term of logic used to denote that when one generally accepted truth is shown to be a cause, another particular effect must necessarily follow.

AB INITIO: From the beginning; a condition which has existed throughout, as in a marriage which was void ab initio.

ACTUS REUS: The wrongful act; in criminal law, such action sufficient to trigger criminal liability.

AD VALOREM: According to value; an ad valorem tax is imposed upon an item located within the taxing jurisdiction calculated by the value of such item.

AMICUS CURIAE: Friend of the court. Its most common usage takes the form of an amicus curiae brief, filed by a person who is not a party to an action but is nonetheless allowed to offer an argument supporting his legal interests.

ARGUENDO: In arguing. A statement, possibly hypothetical, made for the purpose of argument, is one made arguendo.

BILL QUIA TIMET: A bill to quiet title (establish ownership) to real property.

BONA FIDE: True, honest, or genuine. May refer to a person's legal position based on good faith or lacking notice of fraud (such as a bona fide purchaser for value) or to the authenticity of a particular document (such as a bona fide last will and testament).

CAUSA MORTIS: With approaching death in mind. A gift causa mortis is a gift given by a party who feels certain that death is imminent.

CAVEAT EMPTOR: Let the buyer beware. This maxim is reflected in the rule of law that a buyer purchases at his own risk because it is his responsibility to examine, judge, test, and otherwise inspect what he is buying.

CERTIORARI: A writ of review. Petitions for review of a case by the United States Supreme Court are most often done by means of a writ of certiorari.

CONTRA: On the other hand. Opposite. Contrary to.

CORAM NOBIS: Before us; writs of error directed to the court that originally rendered the judgment.

CORAM VOBIS: Before you; writs of error directed by an appellate court to a lower court to correct a factual error.

CORPUS DELICTI: The body of the crime; the requisite elements of a crime amounting to objective proof that a crime has been committed.

CUM TESTAMENTO ANNEXO, ADMINISTRATOR (ADMINISTRATOR C.T.A.): With will annexed; an administrator c.t.a. settles an estate pursuant to a will in which he is not appointed.

DE BONIS NON, ADMINISTRATOR (ADMINISTRATOR D.B.N.): Of goods not administered; an administrator d.b.n. settles a partially settled estate.

DE FACTO: In fact; in reality; actually. Existing in fact but not officially approved or engendered.

DE JURE: By right; lawful. Describes a condition that is legitimate "as a matter of law," in contrast to the term "de facto," which connotes something existing in fact but not legally sanctioned or authorized. For example, de facto segregation refers to segregation brought about by housing patterns, etc., whereas de jure segregation refers to segregation created by law.

DE MINIMUS: Of minimal importance; insignificant; a trifle; not worth bothering about.

DE NOVO: Anew; a second time; afresh. A trial de novo is a new trial held at the appellate level as if the case originated there and the trial at a lower level had not taken place.

DICTA: Generally used as an abbreviated form of obiter dicta, a term describing those portions of a judicial opinion incidental or not necessary to resolution of the specific question before the court. Such nonessential statements and remarks are not considered to be binding precedent.

DUCES TECUM: Refers to a particular type of writ or subpoena requesting a party or organization to produce certain documents in their possession.

EN BANC: Full bench. Where a court sits with all justices present rather than the usual quorum.

EX PARTE: For one side or one party only. An ex parte proceeding is one undertaken for the benefit of only one party, without notice to, or an appearance by, an adverse party.

EX POST FACTO: After the fact. An ex post facto law is a law that retroactively changes the consequences of a prior act.

EX REL.: Abbreviated form of the term ex relatione, meaning, upon relation or information. When the state brings an action in which it has no interest against an individual at the instigation of one who has a private interest in the matter.

FORUM NON CONVENIENS: Inconvenient forum. Although a court may have jurisdiction over the case, the action should be tried in a more conveniently located court, one to which parties and witnesses may more easily travel, for example.

GUARDIAN AD LITEM: A guardian of an infant as to litigation, appointed to represent the infant and pursue his/her rights.

HABEAS CORPUS: You have the body. The modern writ of habeas corpus is a writ directing that a person (body) being detained (such as a prisoner) be brought before the court so that the legality of his detention can be judicially ascertained.

IN CAMERA: In private, in chambers. When a hearing is held before a judge in his chambers or when all spectators are excluded from the courtroom.

IN FORMA PAUPERIS: In the manner of a pauper. A party who proceeds in forma pauperis because of his poverty is one who is allowed to bring suit without liability for costs.

INFRA: Below, under. A word referring the reader to a later part of a book. (The opposite of supra.)

IN LOCO PARENTIS: In the place of a parent.

IN PARI DELICTO: Equally wrong; a court of equity will not grant requested relief to an applicant who is in pari delicto, or as much at fault in the transactions giving rise to the controversy as is the opponent of the applicant.

IN PARI MATERIA: On like subject matter or upon the same matter. Statutes relating to the same person or things are said to be in pari materia. It is a general rule of statutory construction that such statutes should be construed together, i.e., looked at as if they together constituted one law.

IN PERSONAM: Against the person. Jurisdiction over the person of an individual.

IN RE: In the matter of. Used to designate a proceeding involving an estate or other property.

IN REM: A term that signifies an action against the res, or thing. An action in rem is basically one that is taken directly against property, as distinguished from an action in personam, i.e., against the person.

INTER ALIA: Among other things. Used to show that the whole of a statement, pleading, list, statute, etc., has not been set forth in its entirety.

INTER PARTES: Between the parties. May refer to contracts, conveyances or other transactions having legal significance.

INTER VIVOS: Between the living. An inter vivos gift is a gift made by a living grantor, as distinguished from bequests contained in a will, which pass upon the death of the testator.

IPSO FACTO: By the mere fact itself.

JUS: Law or the entire body of law.

LEX LOCI: The law of the place; the notion that the rights of parties to a legal proceeding are governed by the law of the place where those rights arose.

MALUM IN SE: Evil or wrong in and of itself; inherently wrong. This term describes an act that is wrong by its very nature, as opposed to one which would not be wrong but for the fact that there is a specific legal prohibition against it (malum prohibitum).

MALUM PROHIBITUM: Wrong because prohibited, but not inherently evil. Used to describe something that is wrong because it is expressly forbidden by law but that is not in and of itself evil, e.g., speeding.

MANDAMUS: We command. A writ directing an official to take a certain action.

MENS REA: A guilty mind; a criminal intent. A term used to signify the mental state that accompanies a crime or other prohibited act. Some crimes require only a general mens rea (general intent to do the prohibited act), but others, like assault with intent to murder, require the existence of a specific mens rea.

MODUS OPERANDI: Method of operating; generally refers to the manner or style of a criminal in committing crimes, admissible in appropriate cases as evidence of the identity of a defendant.

NEXUS: A connection to.

NISI PRIUS: A court of first impression. A nisi prius court is one where issues of fact are tried before a judge or jury.

N.O.V. (NON OBSTANTE VEREDICTO): Notwithstanding the verdict. A judgment n.o.v. is a judgment given in favor of one party despite the fact that a verdict was returned in favor of the other party, the justification being that the verdict either had no reasonable support in fact or was contrary to law.

NUNC PRO TUNC: Now for then. This phrase refers to actions that may be taken and will then have full retroactive effect.

PENDENTE LITE: Pending the suit; pending litigation underway.

PER CAPITA: By head; beneficiaries of an estate, if they take in equal shares, take per capita.

PER CURIAM: By the court; signifies an opinion ostensibly written "by the whole court" and with no identified author.

PER SE: By itself, in itself; inherently.

PER STIRPES: By representation. Used primarily in the law of wills to describe the method of distribution where a person, generally because of death, is unable to take that which is left to him by the will of another, and therefore his heirs divide such property between them rather than take under the will individually.

PRIMA FACIE: On its face, at first sight. A prima facie case is one that is sufficient on its face, meaning that the evidence supporting it is adequate to establish the case until contradicted or overcome by other evidence.

PRO TANTO: For so much; as far as it goes. Often used in eminent domain cases when a property owner receives partial payment for his land without prejudice to his right to bring suit for the full amount he claims his land to be worth.

QUANTUM MERUIT: As much as he deserves. Refers to recovery based on the doctrine of unjust enrichment in those cases in which a party has rendered valuable services or furnished materials that were accepted and enjoyed by another under circumstances that would reasonably notify the recipient that the rendering party expected to be paid. In essence, the law implies a contract to pay the reasonable value of the services or materials furnished.

QUASI: Almost like; as if; nearly. This term is essentially used to signify that one subject or thing is almost analogous to another but that material differences between them do exist. For example, a quasi-criminal proceeding is one that is not strictly criminal but shares enough of the same characteristics to require some of the same safeguards (e.g., procedural due process must be followed in a parol hearing).

QUID PRO QUO: Something for something. In contract law, the consideration, something of value, passed between the parties to render the contract binding.

RES GESTAE: Things done; in evidence law, this principle justifies the admission of a statement that would otherwise be hearsay when it is made so closely to the event in question as to be said to be a part of it, or with such spontaneity as not to have the possibility of falsehood.

RES IPSA LOQUITUR: The thing speaks for itself. This doctrine gives rise to a rebuttable presumption of negligence when the instrumentality causing the injury was within the exclusive control of the defendant, and the injury was one that does not normally occur unless a person has been negligent.

RES JUDICATA: A matter adjudged. Doctrine which provides that once a court of competent jurisdiction has rendered a final judgment or decree on the merits, that judgment or decree is conclusive upon the parties to the case and prevents them from engaging in any other litigation on the points and issues determined therein.

RESPONDEAT SUPERIOR: Let the master reply. This doctrine holds the master liable for the wrongful acts of his servant (or the principal for his agent) in those cases in which the servant (or agent) was acting within the scope of his authority at the time of the injury.

STARE DECISIS: To stand by or adhere to that which has been decided. The common law doctrine of stare decisis attempts to give security and certainty to the law by following the policy that once a principle of law as applicable to a certain set of facts has been set forth in a decision, it forms a precedent which will subsequently be followed, even though a different decision might be made were it the first time the question had arisen. Of course, stare decisis is not an inviolable principle and is departed from in instances where there is good cause (e.g., considerations of public policy led the Supreme Court to disregard prior decisions sanctioning segregation).

SUPRA: Above. A word referring a reader to an earlier part of a book.

ULTRA VIRES: Beyond the power. This phrase is most commonly used to refer to actions taken by a corporation that are beyond the power or legal authority of the corporation.

ADDENDUM OF FRENCH DERIVATIVES

IN PAIS: Not pursuant to legal proceedings.

CHATTEL: Tangible personal property.

CY PRES: Doctrine permitting courts to apply trust funds to purposes not expressed in the trust but necessary to carry out the settlor's intent.

PER AUTRE VIE: For another's life; in property law, an estate may be granted that will terminate upon the death of someone other than the grantee.

PROFIT A PRENDRE: A license to remove minerals or other produce from land.

VOIR DIRE: Process of questioning jurors as to their predispositions about the case or parties to a proceeding in order to identify those jurors displaying bias or prejudice.

REV 1-95

CASENOTE LEGAL BRIEFS

Administrative Law .... Asimow, Bonfield, & Levin
Administrative Law .... Breyer, Stewart, Sunstein & Spitzer
Administrative Law .... Cass, Diver & Beermann
Administrative Law .... Funk, Shapiro & Weaver
Administrative Law .... Reese
Administrative Law .... Mashaw, Merrill & Shane
Administrative Law .... Strauss, Rakoff, Schotland & Farina (Gellhorn & Byse)
Agency & Partnership .... Hynes
Antitrust .... Handler, Pitofsky, Goldschmid & Wood
Antitrust .... Sullivan & Hovenkamp
Banking Law .... Macey & Miller
Bankruptcy .... Jordan, Warren & Bussel
Bankruptcy .... Warren & Westbrook
Business Organizations .... Cary & Eisenberg (Abridged & Unabridged)
Business Organizations .... Choper, Coffee & Gilson
Business Organizations .... Hamilton
Business Organizations .... Klein, Ramseyer & Bainbridge
Business Organizations .... O'Kelley & Thompson
Business Organizations .... Soderquist, Sommer, Chew & Smiddy
Business Organizations .... Solomon, Schwartz, Bauman & Weiss
Civil Procedure .... Cound, Friedenthal, Miller & Sexton
Civil Procedure .... Field, Kaplan & Clermont
Civil Procedure .... Freer & Perdue
Civil Procedure .... Hazard, Tait & Fletcher
Civil Procedure .... Marcus, Redish & Sherman
Civil Procedure .... Subrin, Minow, Brodin & Main
Civil Procedure .... Yeazell
Commercial Law .... Jordan, Warren & Walt
Commercial Law .... Lopucki, Warren, Keating & Mann
Commercial Law (Sales/Sec.Tr/Pay.Law) .... Speidel, Summers & White
Commercial Law .... Whaley
Community Property .... Bird
Complex Litigation .... Marcus & Sherman
Conflicts .... Brilmayer & Goldsmith
Conflicts .... Cramton, Currie, Kay & Kramer
Conflicts .... Hay, Weintraub & Borchers
Conflicts .... Symeonides, Perdue & Von Mehren
Constitutional Law .... Brest, Levinson, Balkin & Amar
Constitutional Law .... Chemerinsky
Constitutional Law .... Choper, Fallon, Kamisar & Shiffrin (Lockhart)
Constitutional Law .... Cohen & Varat
Constitutional Law .... Farber, Eskridge & Frickey
Constitutional Law .... Rotunda
Constitutional Law .... Sullivan & Gunther
Constitutional Law .... Stone, Seidman, Sunstein & Tushnet
Contracts .... Barnett
Contracts .... Burton
Contracts .... Calamari, Perillo & Bender
Contracts .... Crandall & Whaley
Contracts .... Dawson, Harvey & Henderson
Contracts .... Farnsworth & Young
Contracts .... Fuller & Eisenberg
Contracts .... Knapp, Crystal & Prince
Contracts .... Murphy, Speidel & Ayres
Contracts .... Rosett
Copyright .... Goldstein
Copyright .... Joyce. Patry, Leaffer & Jaszi
Criminal Law .... Bonnie, Coughlin, Jeffries & Low
Criminal Law .... Boyce & Perkins
Criminal Law .... Dressler
Criminal Law .... Johnson
Criminal Law .... Kadish & Schulhofer
Criminal Law .... Kaplan, Weisberg & Binder
Criminal Procedure .... Allen, Kuhns & Stuntz
Criminal Procedure .... Dressler & Thomas
Criminal Procedure .... Haddad, Zagel, Starkman & Bauer
Criminal Procedure .... Kamisar, La Fave & Israel
Criminal Procedure .... Saltzburg & Capra
Criminal Procedure .... Weinreb
Employment Discrimination .... Friedman & Strickler
Employment Discrimination .... Zimmer, Sullivan, Richards & Calloway
Employment Law .... Rothstein, Knapp & Liebman
Environmental Law .... Menell & Stewart
Environmental Law .... Percival, Miller, Schroder & Leape
Environmental Law .... Plater, Abrams, Goldfarb & Graham

Evidence .... Mueller & Kirkpatrick
Evidence .... Strong, Broun & Mousteller
Evidence .... Sutton & Wellborn
Evidence .... Waltz & Park
Evidence .... Weinstein, Mansfield, Abrams & Berger
Family Law .... Areen
Family Law .... Ellman, Kurtz & Bartlett
Family Law .... Harris & Teitelbaum
Family Law .... Krause, Oldham, Elrod & Garrison
Family Law .... Wadlington & O'Brien
Family Law .... Weisberg & Appleton
Federal Courts .... Fallon, Meltzer & Shapiro (Hart & Wechsler)
Federal Courts .... Low & Jeffries
Federal Courts .... Redish & Sherry
First Amendment .... Shiffrin & Choper
Gender and Law .... Bartlett & Harris
Health Care Law .... Curran, Hall, Bobinski & Orentlicher
Health Law .... Furrow, Greaney, Johnson, Jost & Schwartz
Immigration Law .... Aleinikoff, Martin, & Motomura
Immigration Law .... Legomsky
Indian Law .... Getches, Wilkinson & Williams
Insurance Law .... Abraham
Intellectual Property .... Merges, Menell & Lemley
International Business Transactions .... Folsom, Gordon & Spanogle
International Law .... Carter & Trimble
International Law .... Damrosch, Henkin, Pugh, Schachter & Smit
International Law .... Firmage, Blakesley, Scott & Williams (Sweeny & Oliver)
Labor Law .... Cox, Bok, Gorman & Finkin
Land Use .... Callies, Freilich & Roberts
Legislation .... Eskridge, Fricky & Garrett
Mass Media .... Franklin & Anderson
Oil & Gas .... Kuntz, Lowe, Anderson, Smith & Pierce
Patent Law .... Adelman, Radner, Thomas & Wegner
Patent Law .... Francis & Collins
Products Liability .... Owen, Montgomery & Keeton
Professional Responsibility .... Gillers
Professional Responsibility .... Hazard, Koniak & Cramton
Professional Responsibility .... Morgan & Rotunda
Professional Responsibility .... Schwartz, Wydick & Perscbacher
Property .... Casner, Leach, French, Korngold & Vandervelde
Property .... Cribbet, Johnson, Findley & Smith
Property .... Donahue, Kauper & Martin
Property .... Dukeminier & Krier
Property .... Haar & Liebman
Property .... Kurtz & Hovenkamp
Property .... Nelson, Stoebuck & Whitman
Property .... Rabin & Kwall
Property .... Singer
Real Estate .... Berger & Johnstone
Real Estate .... Goldstein & Korngold
Real Estate .... Nelson & Whitman
Remedies .... Bauman & York (Rendleman)
Remedies .... Laycock
Remedies .... Leavell, Love, Nelson & Kovacic-Fleisher
Remedies .... Re & Re
Remedies .... Shoben & Tabb
Securities Regulation .... Cox, Hillman & Langevoort
Securities Regulation .... Jennings, Marsh & Coffee
Sports Law .... Weiler/Roberts
Sports Law .... Yasser
Taxation (Corporate) .... Lind, Schwartz, Lathrope & Rosenberg
Taxation (Estate & Gift) .... Bitker, Clark & McCouch
Taxation (Individual) .... Burke & Friel
Taxation (Individual) .... Freeland, Lind, Stephens & Lathrope
Taxation (Individual) .... Graetz & Schenk
Taxation (Individual) .... Klein, Bankman & Shaviro
Torts .... Dobbs & Hayden
Torts .... Epstein
Torts .... Franklin & Rabin
Torts .... Henderson, Pearson & Siliciano
Torts .... Wade, Schwartz, Kelly & Partlett (Prosser)
Wills, Trusts & Estates .... Clark, Lusky, Murphy, Aascher & McCouch
Wills, Trusts & Estates .... Dukeminier & Johanson
Wills, Trusts & Estates .... Ritchie, Alford & Effland (Dobris & Sterk)
Wills, Trusts & Estates .... Scoles, Halbach, Link & Roberts